Scientists as Entrepreneurs

Organizational Performance In Scientist-Started New Ventures

Scientists as Entrepreneurs

Organizational Performance in Scientist-Started New Ventures

Karel J. Samsom

Nijenrode Universiteit, The Netherlands School of Business
Saint Michael's College, Graduate Business Studies, Vermont,
University of Vermont, School of Business Administration

Kluwer Academic Publishers
Boston/Dordrecht/London

338·04
519₂

Distributors for North America:
Kluwer Academic Publishers
101 Philip Drive
Assinippi Park
Norwell, Massachusetts 02061 USA

Distributors for all other countries:
Kluwer Academic Publishers Group
Distribution Centre
Post Office Box 322
3300 AH Dordrecht, THE NETHERLANDS

Library of Congress Cataloging-in-Publication Data

Samsom, Karel J.
   Scientists as entrepreneurs : organizational
performance in scientist-started new ventures / Karel J. Samsom.
     p. cm.
    ISBN 0-7923-9111-X
    1. New business enterprises—Management. 2. Entrepreneurship.
3. Scientists. I. Title.
HD62.5.S26 1990
338'.04—dc20   90-33719
                                         CIP

Printed in the United States of America

To

Maria & Jan

Lorraine

Caroline & Kaj

three generations of
loving support

CONTENTS

PART II
SCIENTISTS AS ENTREPRENEURS:
THE FIELD STUDIES

PART III
CONCLUSIONS, IMPLICATIONS AND GUIDELINES

FIGURES AND TABLES

PREFACE

"When you are doing something that is a brand new adventure, breaking new ground, whether it is something like a technological breakthrough or simply a way of living that is not what the community can help you with, there is always the danger of too much enthusiasm, of neglecting certain mechanical details. Then you fall off. 'A danger path this is.' When you follow the path of your desire and enthusiasm and emotion, keep your mind in control, and don't let it pull you compulsively into disaster."

Joseph Campbell, The Power of Myth

Through ten years of working with and observing scientists in the biomedical fields, I have found Joseph Campbell's words to be especially applicable to the scientist who decides to embark on an entrepreneurial journey. Joseph Campbell was not a student of entrepreneurship. His scholarship was contained in a series of comprehensive studies of mythology, the captivating stories of mankind's search over the ages for truth, meaning and significance. Still, his advice here contains many of the essential ingredients of successful science-based venturing: the charting of new ground socially, technological breakthroughs, enthusiasm and emotion balanced by careful reasoning, and finally, awareness of the danger of neglecting details.

Coming from such a different philosophical and occupational culture into entrepreneurship and business, the scientist faces extraordinary challenges although the rewards of putting together a successful company can be equally satisfying. Through his transfer of applied knowledge and involvement in its commercialization, the scientist's contributions to society can be significant! Particularly in Canada and the United States, and occasionally in Europe, I have, over the years, observed increasing numbers of scientists embarking on such journeys. A review of the literature on this subject turned up little material specific to the situation of the scientist who becomes an entrepreneur and I decided therefore to undertake a research project covering this subject.

This personal journey of exploration has been both a privilege and a pleasure. As a researcher and a teacher, my purpose was to contribute to the development of a body of knowledge on the subject of the scientist-entrepeneur and his venture. As a practitioner of entrepreneurship, I aimed to produce an initial set of guidelines which could be of direct use to the aspiring scientist who wants to try his hand at venture building. Parts I and II of this book describe and analyze the literature review as well as the original field studies I undertook among scientist-turned-entrepreneurs in Canada and the U.S. Part III offers a summary and conclusions as well as some practical guidelines and checklists which scientists, business partners, financiers, venture capitalist and universities may use to plan their involvement with these types of ventures. I plan to update this latter section from time to time and I welcome any suggestions from practitioners and students of science-based entrepreneurship to improve and elaborate upon these guidelines and checklists. Inasmuch as no female scientists were encountered among the scientists contacted and studied, I have used masculine pronouns throughout this book.

This project has also allowed me to reconnect with the academic community through research associations and teaching, an attractive learning experience I heartily recommend to any businessperson in the middle of his or her career. I have made arrangements to match my personal entrepreneurial and consulting work with ongoing research and teaching activities in this challenging area of study.

I am most grateful for the patient encouragement and assistance I received from Professor Gerard B.J. Bomers, Nijenrode Universiteit, The Netherlands School of Business as well as from Professor Michael A. Gurdon, School of Business Administration, University of Vermont. Dr. Gurdon also cooperated in testing the interview instrument and in the conduct of the field studies in Vermont and Quebec. Gerard Bomers, Michael Gurdon and I further co-authored a number of related articles. My warmest thanks to you both! What would we have done without fax machines?

My thanks go also to Professor Anthonie Wattel who originally encouraged me to transfer to the Wharton School of Finance and Commerce, University of Pennsylvania at a time when there were still no business schools in Europe and who, more recently, helped me in starting this project. With their constructive comments and support, Professors Savitt and Wetzel at the University of Vermont and the University of New Hampshire respectively, helped me stay on track with this research study. Then there are my students in the entre-preneurship and innovation courses at Burlington College and Saint Michael's College, Graduate Business Studies, in Vermont who often unwittingly provided a constructive platform for discussing some of the concepts in this book.

I would further like to express my appreciation to my former colleagues, both executives and scientists, at Eli Lilly and Company, Alcon Laboratories and Psychemedics Corporation who provided me with the experiences which eventually led to the inspiration to write this book. In particular, I want to mention Dr. Frederic Lloyd, Robert Barkei, William Miller, Allen Baker, Timothy Sear and Dr. Werner Baumgartner who, in various ways, helped me prepare for and facilitated my own venturing aspirations! A special word of thanks goes to my friend Dale Cummings whose insights significantly added to my understanding of the personal and psychological characteristics of scientists and who, on occasion, reminded me to see my journey in this area with a sense of humor!

The scientists and clinicians who contributed many hours of their precious time to participate in this study, deserve a very special mention here. They shared their personal entrepreneurial experience, successes and failures, and are individually recognized with their ventures in Table 4-1. Their team members also participated in the completion of the field studies.

Finally, I would like to mention Lorraine B. Good, my best partner in more than one way, William Folmar and Michael Gurdon, masters of the English language, Michael Spillane, the artist who skillfully created the cover, and Frederik Parmentier, Jan, Ingeborg and Koos Samsom, Netherlands-based supporters and organizers! They should know that, in their own special way, they helped me in the completion of this study. Beware, I have more research and writing plans!

Burlington, Vermont, March 1990   K.J.S.

Scientists as Entrepreneurs

Organizational Performance In Scientist-Started New Ventures

Part I

Introduction, Research and Methodology

Chapter 1

AN INTRODUCTION TO SCIENTISTS AS ENTREPRENEURS

1.1 The Research Problem

I was originally drawn to the study of the activities of scientists in the medical and related technologies who are involved in the commercial application of their own inventions, when I was affiliated as an executive with Alcon Laboratories of Fort Worth, Texas. Alcon Laboratories is a multinational corporation with its main activities in the development and commercialization of medical and pharmaceutical products related to health care for the human eye. This interest continued during my subsequent work as president of Psychemedics Corporation, a new business venture based on a scientific invention in the research and clinical diagnostic testing field. I therefore observed, and was on occasion involved in, the start-up processes of a number of entrepreneurial and intrapreneurial ventures involving scientists. In these types of new product ventures, whether established as independent firms or within existing corporations, both success and failure can be witnessed. Nonetheless, it also appears that, irrespective of business performance, these inventions often provide major successes and breakthroughs from a scientific or technological point of view. Thus, technological success is not automatically synonymous with business success. A corollary observation is that in the very process of commercialization, the technology can be damaged or lost.

Why do scientists want to become involved in the commercialization processes of their ideas? How would they proceed to implement their designs through business activities? How do they retain their relationships with academic or research institutions? What are some of the important determinants of their success or failure? These are just some of the initial questions I posed concerning the concept of scientists involved with entrepreneurship.

Although I have witnessed clinicians and scientists in European countries who were involved in such entrepreneurial endeavors, my own observations and my reading of the business press indicate that this is *still* predominantly a North American phenomenon, with the possible exception of the United Kingdom. One of my early and intuitive inclinations was that a key factor affecting business performance appeared to be the degree to which these commercially involved scientists were effectively able to switch continually from academic research and development settings to business environments and back again. Fascinated with this phenomenon in innovation--its problems as well as its opportunities--I set out to conduct a research project on this subject.

The process of commercializating technological developments and inventions through new ventures is a phenomenon occurring routinely in the business environments. I am referring here to the rather standard procedure wherein a scientist from a university, independent institution, or government research and development facility produces a scientific and technological inno- vation. At some point, the discovery is recognized to have sufficient application potential outside the laboratory to justify an attempt at commercialization. At this stage, the organization of a new commercial venture typically separates the particular inventor-scientist from the technological breakthrough in question through the transfer to the firm of all data defining the invention. Increasingly, however, the scientist in question decides to be affiliated with the new venture. In such cases the scientist will assist in or direct any or all of the developmental stages from the research laboratory through to a marketed product or service. The type of relationship in which such an affiliation might be structured is typically as an entrepreneur, partner, shareholder, or consultant, and usually involves a combination of these roles. The critical departure from his academic endeavors lies in the fact that the scientist now becomes involved in the management of entrepreneurial processes, including risking personal resources invested in the venture. The scientists studied in this research have thus become real entrepreneurs!

The research problem driving this study, therefore, consists of the following elements:

1. Develop a theoretical framework in which the specific aspects of scientist-started new business ventures can be studied.

2. Conduct empirical research among a number of scientist-started new business ventures.

3. Evaluate the results of this research; propose suggestions for further research and for the improvement of start-up procedures for the scientist-initiated venture.

1.2 Purpose and Perspective

The intensity with which change can confront the scientist who opens up his career experiences to an entirely new field can be dramatic. When a scientist who previously had a career involved primarily in research and development at a university, or an independent or government research laboratory, decides to play a substantial role in the commercializing venture, he is soon faced with a completely new set of work-related challenges and opportunities. *The theory and practice of setting up new business ventures present realities that are entirely different from the research and development environments from which the scientist has come.*

To *begin* to specifically explain and understand the performance of scientist-started new business ventures, we can study existing literature and research on scientists' characteristics, academic cultures, management and organization, innovation, technology transfer and entrepreneurship. To further deepen our understanding of this phenomenon, however, original exploratory research among scientist-started new business ventures needs to be carried out.

Entrepreneurship is a multidisciplinairy field of study. When the scientist-started nature of entrepreneurship is added, even more points of view appear that can be adopted in exploring this subject. I have listed below some of the major issues that can arise:

- opportunities and conflicts in industry-university relationships,
- technology transfer,
- psychological, behavioral, and socioeconomic characteristics of scientists,
- differences between scientific and entrepreneurial "cultures,"
- innovation,

- research and development management,
- organization and management,
- finance and funding,
- entrepreneurship processes,
- the role of entrepreneurship in the economy.

All these individual topics could lead to fascinating studies in their own right. Chapter 2 provides a number of basic but widely used definitions that will delineate this research and guide it through comprehensive field studies. My aim in defining the research perspective was to focus on exploring those performance variables in *the planning and initial management stages* which were *specific* to the scientist-started nature of the venture. In focusing on the aspects that were *specific* to the scientist-started nature of the venture, the opportunity was presented to conduct *original* research. Finally, it has been an important objective from the inception of this study to develop, on the basis of this research, a practical model or framework that could provide some guidance to aspiring scientist-entrepreneurs and their business partners in the early stages of their venturing activities.

Thus, while this study occasionally draws from a wide array of fields as defined above, the primary perspective applied is that of the organizational and management aspects of entrepreneurial processes in scientist-started ventures. A secondary theme relates to the nature of university-scientist relationships. Finally, some of the findings of this research in related areas, such as socio-economic variables and comparative management, will also be reported.

In summary, the purpose of this research project is to develop *theoretical* and *practical* frameworks for the study of the scientist-started new business venture. It aims to identify and develop an improved understanding of the specific challenges and opportunities facing these kinds of start-up companies and, where appropriate, it will suggest strategies for such new ventures.

1.3   Organization of the Study

This study has been organized into three major parts:

Part I, **Introduction, Research, and Methodology**, is comprised of chapters 1 through 3. In chapter 2, I will complete a literature review of a number of works relevant to the study of *organization and management processes* *in the scientist-started venture.* This review will assist in the definition of an instrument for the field studies and the subsequent analysis. Chapter 3 describes the qualitative research methodology adopted in the design, conduct and analysis of the field studies among 22 scientist-started ventures in the States of Massachusetts, Maine, New Hampshire, Vermont and the Provinces of Ontario and Quebec.

Part II, **The Field Studies**, is comprised of chapters 4 through 6 and reports the findings of the empirical studies. In chapter 4, socioeconomic data from the studies will be evaluated in terms of earlier relevant research in Canada and the United States. Chapter 5 will present and analyze the entrepreneurial, organization and management aspects of the field studies. Chapter 6 presents some additional findings in the areas of industry-university and scientist-university relationships, and also provides a comparative analysis of the Canadian and United States enterprises.

Part III, **Conclusions, Implications and Guidelines**, presents some theoretical as well as practical conclusions which arise from this exploratory study. Chapter 7 summarizes the findings of both literature and field studies, presents conclusions, and discusses the applicability of this work. The final chapter, chapter 8, offers an initial framework for scientist-entrepreneurs and their business partners as a guide for effective venture planning and early management processes.

Chapter 2

AN OVERVIEW OF THE RESEARCH LITERATURE RELATED TO SCIENTIST-STARTED VENTURES

2.1 Introduction

In this chapter I will review the relevant research literature that assist in exploring the phenomenon of the scientist-turned-entrepreneur and his venture. Where appropriate, I will also draw conclusions and formulate a research framework and some propositions which will be the basis for the field work described in part II of this study. Chapter 2 is further organized as follows:

In chapter 1, scientist-started business ventures were identified as a sub-group of the general category of entrepreneurial ventures. Small business and entrepreneurship research has surged in recent years, particularly in the United States, as evidence mounted that new ventures were contributing a far greater share to the overall growth of the economy than had previously been recognized. Particularly dramatic were findings with respect to job creation by new ventures. Acs and Audretsch summarized these as follows:

> Twenty years ago it hardly seemed that small firms would emerge as the engine for generating new jobs in the U.S. Certainly at that time the preoccupation of the literature in industrial economics was with identifying the extent of concentration in markets and its effects on economic performance. Yet, small enterprises did create the majority of new U.S. employment over the ensuing two decades, both in manufacturing as well as for the entire economy.[1]

There are no specific statistics published in Canada or the United States on the number of annual high-technology company formations, nor are there on those initiated by scientists. However, considering the high incidence of reports and case studies of start-ups in computer technology and the biomedical fields during the last two decades, I believe we may conclude that the number of new high-tech ventures has also increased significantly during the same period. Dubinskas[2] reported in 1985 that in the major centers of biotechnology activity --Boston, San Francisco and Washington--some 200 genetic engineering companies had been formed since 1980. With the increase in new high-tech firms, the phenomenon of the scientist as entrepreneur, the subject of this study, has become more common.

The research that has been conducted on entrepreneurship has been grouped by one set of authors, Paulin, Coffey, and Spaulding,[3] into four main themes:

1. The entrepreneur as an individual.
2. The process or mechanics of entrepreneurship.
3. The functions of entrepreneurship in society.
4. Supporting topics.

The place of entrepreneurship in society is outside the scope of this research study. My research concentrates primarily on the first two topics listed. The objective is to study a particular type of entrepreneur, his background and motivations, and how he functions within the entrepreneurial and organizational processes. In this study, that entrepreneur is a scientist by experience, training and education, as opposed to a businessperson or other kind of individual starting a new business venture. Within this area of the individual entrepreneur, Paulin, Coffey, and Spaulding[4] further propose three approaches: case histories describing individual scientist-entrepreneurs, sociological studies defining socio-economic characteristics of entrepreneurs, and the psychological approach to understanding the entrepreneur.

As far as case histories are concerned, I have found no systematic and comparative descriptions of multiple cases of scientists as entrepreneurs. Chapter 5 will start to fill this void in reporting on the entrepreneurial profiles generated during the field studies in Canada and the United States among 22 scientist-entrepreneurs and their ventures. Chapter 4 reviews the socioeconomic background characteristics of the these entrepreneurs and evaluates our findings in the light of earlier studies of technical entrepreneurs.

2.2   Definitions

Such terms as *venture, entrepreneur, scientific method, scientist, technology, invention, innovation* and *scientist-started business* are central to this study. These are all terms that are used frequently and in many settings. A discussion of their various definitions as they have evolved in the literature could be the subject of a separate research project. To assure a common basis of both practical and theoretical understanding, I have, in this research, used Webster's Ninth New Collegiate Dictionary (Merriam-Webster, 1988) for the definitions. Where necessary, these definitions will be further developed in the course of this chapter.

Entrepreneur: "one who organizes, manages, and assumes the risk of a business or enterprise."

Innovation: "the introduction of something new."

Invention: "a device, contrivance, or process originated after study and experiment."

Scientific method: "principles and procedures for the systematic pursuit of knowledge involving the recognition and formulation of a problem, the collection of data through observation and experiment, and the formulation and testing of hypotheses."

Scientist: "one learned in science and especially natural science: a scientific investigator."

Technology: "applied science; a scientific method of achieving a practical purpose; the totality of the means employed to provide objects necessary for human sustenance and comfort."

Venture: "an undertaking involving chance, risk, or danger; especially a speculative business enterprise."

Variations on these general definitions are used in the English language. For instance, the term *venture* is used, certainly within the business culture, to emphasize risk-taking, rather than merely chance or speculation. My use of the term *scientist* agrees with the definition, with the added specification that scientists discussed here would usually be university trained, and their previous associations would have been primarily with government or university research and development activities. E.B. Roberts'[5] definition of invention and innovation processes holds that *innovation equals invention plus exploitation,* and I will return to this useful concept. With these additions, the definitions given above are used in this study as the most generally accepted ones. The term, *scientist-started venture,* is further elaborated as follows.

Two principal differences exist between new company start-ups in general and ventures that are originated by scientists. In the first place, as implied in the definition of scientist-started entrepreneurial activities, such businesses are usually based on scientific innovations, developments, or refinements as incorporated in their products or services. The business thus has a comparatively high technological content. The second distinction lies in the fact that, at least initially, the commercialization effort is started and is partially or fully controlled by a specific type of entrepreneur whose past experience, unlike the general entrepreneur, has been primarily as a scientist in training, experience, and outlook.

The first difference--the presence of high technology innovation--is not unique in itself. Technology-based innovation in existing organizations has been studied widely. It is the combination of technological innovation with the scientist-initiated and driven organization, which provides a unique area of study. The process of venture planning and management, in which the founding scientist plays a major or controlling role in the commercialization of his technology has not been the subject of much management research. Yet, it appears from the business press and research literature and is also underscored by my own observations that substantial growth in scientist-started ventures in the biotechnology and medical fields has taken place in recent years. Whether these two combined differences with the general population of business start-ups are to be considered as differences in degree or as differences in principle, thus requiring a different theoretical and practical approach, is one of the questions that this study aims to answer.

2.3   Scientists' Characteristics

This section examines whether available knowledge concerning scientists' behavioral and attitudinal characteristics could be of assistance in effectively explaining the creation and organizational processes of scientist-started business ventures. I depart here from the assumption that the scientist, having invented or developed some technology which might have commercial application, has decided to play a central role in planning and/or implementing the venture. Thus, the particular scientist in each venture is a given with certain background and personality characteristics. As implied in the introductory section, this study was not designed to investigate socioeconomic data which analyze common background statistics of entrepreneurs, although some of these aspects, as found in the field studies, will be reviewed in chapter 4. The main objective is to explore a theory which could start to explain the behavioral and organizational aspects of the phenomenon of the scientist-started new business venture.

It has often been postulated that scientists as a group tend to possess personal characteristics which are different from those of non-scientists. In this connection, the studies reviewed below deal with scientists and sometimes engineers in technology-based fields of scientific endeavor, such as physics, engineering, biology, chemistry, and medicine. To what extent these characteristics vary among those different scientific fields is not known and would require further study. For the purpose of exploring the science-based venture, this general definition would be sufficient. Following this line of reasoning, understanding the behavioral and attitudinal differences between scientists and non-scientists could assist in explaining the planning and management actions of scientist-entrepreneurs and their influence on business performance.

L.E. Danielson, in Characteristics of Engineers and Scientists,[6] reports on a study of 277 nonsupervisory and 90 supervisory scientists and engineers in industrial organizations. The findings are derived from the self-reported perceptions of participants. The majority of the participants reported some major perceived differences between other employees and themselves. Scientists and engineers saw themselves as follows:

- more persistent,
- more objective and skeptical,
- more responsible,
- dedicated to fundamental knowledge in addition to organization loyalty,
- more individualistic,
- more creative,
- striving for broader, higher goals,

It would not be unreasonable to suppose that such differences, whether perceived or objectively measured, if not recognized, could initiate the development of different cultures within the organization, and potentially lead to a lack of identification by all employees with common venture values and objectives.

Frank A. Dubinskas, an anthropologist who spent two years observing scientists and managers in biotechnology companies, arrives at a similar conclusion of substantial cultural differences between the two groups.[7] According to Dubinskas, managers are more short-term and specific goal oriented, while scientists focus on longer planning periods and broader, less limiting goals. Investor pressure and the demands of quarterly reports are seen to conflict with the attainment of intellectual goals. He concludes that these differences primarily derive from substantially different educational backgrounds.

In a more recent book, Janus Organizations,[8] Dubinskas elaborates on these differences that are perceived to be rooted in the different perceptions of *planning time* and *developmental time*. The manager develops short-term and long-term specific plans and then measures performance against these milestones. This planning and performance management and reporting provide the tools with which the manager relates to his principals and the outside investor. The manager's world is thus very focused and economic goal oriented, and he perceives this as the venture's *reality*. The scientist's work is governed by the laws of nature which are difficult to predict. Goals are much broader, the timing of achievements less predictable and long term in nature. Managers tend to stereotype these attitudes as *"not realistic."* The scientist sees scientific knowledge as primary, with economic goals a secondary consideration. The concept of developmental time shows further how profoundly different managers and scientists can be in their very outlook on life and self perception. In the concept of *developmental time*, managers see themselves as fully formed and developed human beings who may, on that basis, advance further through their executive careers. Scientists tend to see their development as continuous during their entire life span. Their growth never reaches completion as they continue to discover and conquer new scientific puzzles. In addition to these profound cultural differences, each group belongs to a high status profession in the North American environment. Dubinskas' implication is here that without some level of reconciliation through improved communications between these two groups, serious and prolonged conflicts can afflict the venture, and long-term corporate health frequently suffers.

In <u>Winning the Games Scientists Play</u>,[9] Carl J. Sindemann has developed the theme that, for the scientist, relating to industry (as opposed to government or academia) is the more difficult challenge. In industry, there is more demand for commitment to the organization's goals, more financial control and administrative paperwork, and better financial rewards, but also more likelihood of projects being cancelled. These forces can conflict with the scientist's individual characteristics and objectives. Finally, Sindemann concludes: " It may be that scientists, as a group, disagree with the concept of financial gain as the sole reason for existence, or with total pragmatism as an operating philosophy. But whatever the reason, relationships of most scientists with industry must be described as uneasy."

Burns and Stalker,[10] in their early and original work on innovation management, present an organizational perspective on the industrial scientist. Scientists in industry, according to their research, display a semidetached attitude toward the organization as a result of their professional loyalties. The image of the scientist as an eccentric, absentminded but bright professional was also observed to be used often by management as a reason to keep them out of executive roles. Emphasis on the industrial R&D role to the detriment of other activities in a multifunctional firm can, moreover, lead to isolation problems within the organization.

Many students of entrepreneurship have taken an ex-post point of view in identifying characteristics of successful entrepreneurs. From a technological and entrepreneurial point of view, this approach has, for instance, been taken by Roberts and Wainer in "Some Characteristics of Technical Entrepreneurs"[11] and

by Litvak and Maule in "Some Characteristics of Successful Technical
Entrepreneurs In Canada."[12] These studies primarily examined the social,
economic, and ethnic backgrounds of surveyed technical entrepreneurs. As such,
they provide insights into family background, education levels, and entrepreneurial motivation. In chapter 4, we will draw on these findings.

With the exception of the work of Danielson, the studies reviewed here have
relied on undefined numbers of case studies and the authors' personal observations in delineating scientists' attitudes and characteristics. A summary of
these authors' conclusions, including Danielson's report of the research subjects'
self-perceptions, shows a number of common characteristics.

- Cultural differences between scientists and managers, as evidenced by different
  perceptions of time and planning horizons or differing perceptions of
  organizational goals.

- Scientists' implied duality of loyalty in working for a greater cause (general
  scientific knowledge) than just the organizational mission.

- Managers as more pragmatic, purpose oriented than scientists who are more
  objective and display greater skepticism.

- Scientists' long-term orientation versus managers' short-term view of venture
  performance.

- The creative, eccentric, disorganized image of the scientist versus the
  controlled and administratively-oriented manager.

- Scientists' need for control over "their" technology as it transfers to the
  venture and is developed further there.

- Scientists' narrow view of technology as beginning and ending in the
  laboratory; managers see technology merely as *one of many inputs* in the
  commercialization process.

- Scientists' tendency to overrate the importance of technology in the venture.

Personality and other types of attitudinal characterizations of scientists, as
discussed here, have relied on surveys of self-perception and on the observations
of the various authors quoted here. My own experiences in working with and

observing scientists in organizational settings during the last 20 years certainly confirm many elements of these stereotypes. I am further impressed with the significant commonalty of traits that have been observed by an array of researchers from various fields. Even so, further study of scientists' characteristics to confirm and refine these patterns would be helpful. In particular, a study investigating the possible link between the psychological profiles of scientist-entrepreneurs and long-term venture performance would contribute significantly to the study of scientist-started ventures.

It is important to emphasize that none of the studies I identified and reviewed specifically addressed the notion of the scientist-started and -led new business venture. I submit that the leadership requirements made of scientists in firms started by them substantially increase the pitfalls to which the venture *might* be subjected. This prospect is inherent in the differing characteristics of scientists as compared with those of other successful entrepreneurs.

There is a potential conflict in the two roles that the scientist-entrepreneur must play. These roles are further defined in the following section on planning and management. Suffice it to mention here that such conflicts may occur as a result of the differing role demands of being a scientist or scientist-innovator, on the one hand, and an entrepreneur implementing the commercialization processes on the other. This potential for conflict is further increased by the scientist's exposure to power in the organization as a top executive from its inception. Timmons[13] expresses the various role demands conveniently in Figure 2-1.

FIGURE 2-1. The Entrepreneur Versus the Inventor

C R E A T I V I T Y	INVENTOR	ENTREPRENEUR
	BUREAUCRAT	MANAGER

MANAGEMENT SKILLS

From: Timmons et al. New Venture Creation (1985)

So, while I accept the possibility that the characteristics of scientists, as a group, might be substantially different from other groups working in a new venture, I also propose that in order to anticipate the influence these differences will have on the management of the organization, an additional in-depth study of the characteristics and behavior of scientist-entrepreneurs is needed. Part II of this study addresses this question.

The foregoing section can be summarized as follows:

• The generalized picture of scientists' behavioral characteristics presented here could be of value in the planning, staffing, and management process of the new venture in that it provides a checklist of potential interpersonal and cultural hurdles.

• A scientific study of the scientists' personal characteristics, attitudes and motivations in general, and of those scientists who are also entrepreneurs in particular, would contribute to the construction of an objective body of knowledge on the subject.

2.4 Planning and Management in the Scientist-Started New Venture

The initial venture phase studied here can be divided into two distinct time periods: (1) the pre-venture exploration and planning stage, and (2) the initial management phase which starts with the original funding of the enterprise.

Bartunek and Betters-Reed[14] highlight the following critical issues for any organization during the commitment and early planning stage:

• Creativity and thoroughness of the planning process;
• Depth of commitment of the originator and planners to the organization;
• Internal dynamics among originator and planners;
• Quality of planner's relationship with the environment.

As is the case in the establishment of any organization, the decisions made during the scientist's venture planning process form an important variable influencing the business performance during the subsequent life of the venture. For purposes of this study, I have defined the scientist's exploration and planning period to start at such time as he has decided that his technological idea might be ready for funding and possible commercial development, and to end at the time of the formation and initial funding of the venture. In this study I am thus not concerned with the actual process of research and development and technological invention prior to the decision to explore a business venture.

Michael C. Martin,[15] in one of the few innovation management studies published that deal specifically with technologically based innovations and technological entrepreneurs, defines three stages of the technological new venture creation process as follows:

> "Moonlighting" Stage: during this period the technical entrepreneur evolves and plans his venture ideas while remaining on the payroll of an academic or research institution. The emphasis during this period is on technology definition and screening for purposes of obtaining venture capital and the evaluation of market potential.

> Postlaunch Stage: building the organization: securing financial support, developing the manufacturing capability, testing the marketability of the innovative product through market launch.

> Consolidation and Growth to Maturity: "Once the venture has survived the launching period and established itself as at least an initially viable commercial entity, its founders will look to consolidation and possible expansion." [16]

This study deals primarily with the first two stages defined by Martin and is further limited to the specific implications for scientists starting their own ventures. In reviewing current literature on these planning phases, in particular those that address the specific aspects of the scientist-started business venture, I will focus on the venture team, the technology, and the market.

2.4.1   The Venture Team

Martin emphasizes how venture team formation is the most urgent and critical of all these planning tasks. A substantial number of researchers of entrepreneurship express the same or similar conclusions. In venture team formation, technical creativity and entrepreneurship should be optimally combined. Timmons with Smollen and Dingee[17] define the driving forces in new venture creation in terms of (1) The Founders, (2) The Opportunity, and (3) Necessary Resources. They propose that the degree of fit between the elements of these forces influences the success of the venture. Both in the categories of founders and necessary resources we then find, in addition to functional tasks, a need for the development of a capable venture team as one of the key requirements for success. Given acceptable levels of perceived technological achievement and market potential, private investors, venture capitalists and Wall Street alike tend to heavily favor projects that are led by venture teams representing a balanced proportion of all the functional skills necessary to research, develop and commercialize the technological innovation further. Venture capitalists and financiers usually probe the viability of the scientist's innovation, as well as its potential for scaling up and, in this review, test its applicability to known or perceived market demand. However, the underlying evaluation concerns both the functional quality of the venture team as well as the way the members appear to cooperate in a team spirit.

Such an approach to venture team building assists in the definition of the ideal profiles of individual venture management team members. Martin[18] compares this process to the manner in which a pearl grows. The venture team grows around a small and close group of lead entrepreneurs who represent the technological and entrepreneurial aspirations of the firm.

Roberts, in "Influences on Innovation: Extrapolations to Biomedical Technology,"[19] has suggested five types of key roles that need to be played in technological innovation management, based on a review of various studies in innovation management:

- idea-havers: e.g., the scientist;
- idea-exploiters: e.g., the entrepreneur;
- program manager: e.g., nontechnical supportive functions;
- gatekeeper: e.g., the provider of technical, market and manufacturing information for the venture;
- sponsor: e.g., senior mentor to support operational technical staff.

While the scientist-started venture will usually be too small to staff individually for these requirements, the model nevertheless serves as an innovation oriented indication of which specific tasks need to be addressed in the science-based firm.

Drucker,[20] in his recent book on entrepreneurship, makes reference to an often observed attitude of technological executives and entrepreneurs--one which considers anything that is not advanced knowledge, including business training, to be of secondary importance. Litvak and Maule,[21] in their work on successful technical entrepreneurs in Canada, also noted the lack of management skills in technical entrepreneurs as a reason for not seeing the need to hire the required business skills, resulting in an inability to successfully develop and propose business plans for funding purposes. In this area, Sindemann makes the most powerful statement[22] when he notes that the one failing which he has identified in the conversion phase from scientist to scientist-administrator is "the unwillingness of the convert to admit that management training is a critical part of that transition, and (even if it is admitted) unwillingness to carry through with the training."

Staffing the top management levels of biotechnology firms has recently captured the imagination of newspapers and trade journals. Through these channels the public at large and the investment community have become more aware of the phenomenon of the scientist-turned entrepreneur and its impact on high-tech venture performance. The fundamental question asked by these articles is: Should the Chief Executive Officer of a high-tech firm have a scientific background? New England Business[23] reviewed seven biotechnology firms in the Boston area in 1986, and noted that, although there are some exceptions, the majority of the firms were eventually led by businessmen, often senior executives originating in the pharmaceutical industry. This is explained by the need for an executive who has the ability to go from the idea stage to the fully commercialized stage. Bio/Technology[24] dedicated an article to hiring trends in which its editor interviewed a number of executive search firms that specialize in recruiting management employees for biotechnology firms. Their comments appear to reflect a movement among the firms interviewed toward greater organizational maturity with a related shift in executive requirements. While in the seventies and through the mid-eighties, the scientist-entrepreneurs with technologically innovative ideas were able to capture funding for their ventures relatively easily, the notion of the chief scientist running the company has lost its glamour. Companies are looking for managers and administrators, and the top priority for the CEO appears to be an ability to raise money, followed by experience in taking a company from the R&D stage to a full-fledged marketing posture! Finally, companies now require more technological understanding from their nonscientific executives.

The New York Times[25] recently featured an article on a scientist who, nine years after founding the firm, remains its CEO and thus not only successfully made the transition to entrepreneur but, subsequently, also to corporate executive. This CEO has meanwhile stepped back from day-to-day operations and has brought in experienced executives in all functional areas. Five additional biotechnology companies reviewed in the article have turned to veteran managers as chief executive officers. Almost all had significant prior exposure to and experience with high technology.

One of the dominant themes of Moss Kanter's <u>When Giants Learn to Dance</u>[26] is that to support innovation, not only technological but also professional management *and* entrepreneurial skills need to be present in the venture. Although she describes innovation and venture in terms of those in existing corporations, these messages also apply to high technology start-up firms.

The last issue to be addressed in respect to the venture team relates to the role of the founding scientist. Clarity among the members of the venture management team during the planning and management phases concerning the scientist-founder's role and future intent is necessary. In "New Venture Creation: Models and Methodologies", Timmons[27] reviews the work of authors of venture research during the 1970s. In varying degrees and detail these studies commonly emphasize the need for lead entrepreneurs to understand their own objectives, capabilities, characteristics, and skills. Drucker[28] significantly suggests that founders ask themselves the following type of questions regularly and as objectively as possible: What does the organization need in skills? What am I good at? What do I really want to do? Where do I belong? Venture team members will look to the founder for leadership and guidance. Timmons, with Smollen and Dingee,[29] proposes a practical approach to team building based on some of the same questions.

Although none of the studies specifically dealt with the scientist-started firm, this review did provide relevant input into the study of the team formation process in this type of firm.

• Team formation is a critical element in venture development. Innovation requires technological, entrepreneurial, and professional management skills. Founders' goals need to be shared with the venture team.

• In science-based ventures, there is significant potential for technological domination in the venture team.

• Business training tends to be resisted by scientific and technical team members.

• As biomedical firms mature, chief executive positions are increasingly being captured by professional managers.

2.4.2   The Technology

So far in this chapter, I have dealt with two prime variables in the study of the scientist-started new business venture: scientists' characteristics and the venture management team. In the remainder of this chapter I will explore how the planning and management of technological and market developments are specifically affected by the scientist-started nature of the enterprise. Finally, organizational aspects will be evaluated from the same perspective.

In this type of venture I anticipate the absence of, or an abbreviated form of the technology transfer phase. As the scientist "brings" the technology with him into the venture, there will be potentially less formal definition and documentation of the technology at the venture planning and start-up phases. A detailed definition of the state of the technology is desirable since it is the basis for the following activities in the planning and operational phase of the venture:

• acquisition of funding;
• business planning;
• technical development and production, pilot projects;
• research and development, field and demonstration studies;
• market assessment, marketing strategies and segmentation;
• human resources development, training and recruitment.

Drucker recommends careful technology assessment.[30] What additional know-ledge must be obtained to implement the technology and commercialize it? This knowledge might not have to be scientific or technological itself. Drucker uses the example of the Wright brothers who had the plans of a plane and a recently developed engine to propel it but had to work out the missing mathematics of flight in order to succeed. In my own experience in venture management, we had obtained the technology to develop and manufacture a very high gas permeable, semi-rigid contact lens, thus allowing an entirely new group of patients requiring the use of corrective eye glasses to switch to contact lenses. However, it appeared that the team was unable to commercialize this innovation successfully as long as it did not have the know-how to teach substantial numbers of eye doctors in a cost-effective way the procedures to fit these lenses successfully. The contact lens material was the new technology; the additional knowledge required was how to conduct a substantial practitioner training plan effectively and economically. The technology, which was originally defined as polymer science, and the techniques to manufacture these lenses had to be extended to include clinical and organizational know-how to operate an effective practitioner contact lens fitting program.

The possibility exists that the scientist remains preoccupied with what is the technological definition of the development in the strictest sense rather than planning the inclusion of such items as pilot manufacturing, quality control, and test marketing in the light of customer demands. Planning in such ventures is then primarily technology dominated, to the detriment of other functions. Furthermore, the preponderance of technology is often increased by the general acceptance that technological tasks can only be understood, carried out, and supervised by technological staff. These two issues are interrelated.

Dubinskas[31] reports that a ratio of up to four scientists to one nonscientist could be found in the companies he surveyed. Domination of technology can lead to what Martin[32] refers to as Technological Obsession. "Venture teams that are too absorbed in their technology may, in reality, be regressing back to their childhoods, and trying to run their company as a technologically sophisticated toy train set." Timmons et al discuss this problem in terms of the difference between the invention and the opportunity and how it would seem in this rapidly changing world that if the idea were technology based, success would be guaranteed. They conclude:

> The intense and highly ego-involved personal identity and commitment to an invention or new widget tends to weaken, or preclude entirely, realistic assessment of other crucial aspects of the business-- (1) the market potential, (2) the difficulty in developing the product to full completion so that it is ready for the market, (3) the time and effort required to introduce the product and gain customer acceptance, and (4) the real value of the invention--and the failure to make such an assessment can become an obstacle to attracting investors and a management team.[33]

Just as in the case of business training for technologists and scientists, there is a reluctance for nontechnical managers to enter into the field of technology. Yet, particularly in the small technological venture, sizeable commitments of limited resources often have to be made on the basis of technological intricacies.

Unless the full venture management team--scientific and non-scientific members alike--understands the basic implications of technological matters, decisions might turn out destructively for the venture. "Technology and the Manager" by Wickham Skinner[34] addresses with this need. The message of his chapter is that "...industrious managers can learn to understand and to deal effectively with the technology of their industries and that this process is by no means difficult, endless or distracting when approached from a managerial view-point. The conclusion of Skinner is applicable to all technology-based enterprises, but, in my opinion, it is of crucial necessity for small science-based ventures. "In these times of rapid technological change, a manager cannot afford to be technology aversive. Technologies can be analyzed and characterized systemati-cally by the non-engineer/non-scientist. Analogies can be worked out to develop conceptual understandings. The relationship between EPT (equipment and process technology) and its resulting economics and constraints are generally straight-forward, as is the understanding that these three factors will highlight the especially difficult aspects of managing any operations, allowing the manager to focus his or her attention."[35]   In summary, we reviewed the following issues:

• Technology assessment is required to identify further development needs as well as market opportunities.

• When the technology assessment effort is limited to the technologists in the team, the potential exists that this technology will be overemphasized in comparison with its market application.

• Technology training for non-technically trained team members is desirable.

2.4.3   The Market

In this section, specific aspects of the planning for market assessment and marketing will be examined that relate to the situation of scientist-started business ventures. This review is thus not a comprehensive treatise of market-ing in the high-tech new venture, but will focus on the particular impact that the scientist might have on marketing in his venture.

In extremis, the vision of the role of technology in the marketplace is either based on a technology-push or on a market-pull concept. In the case of the former, the available or technologically most advanced product or service is placed in the market and offered as the best that can be made. This is a serious possibility in any technology-dominated new venture. In the market-pull situation, technology domination is ruled out by a process of step-by-step feedback from the market during the technology development process as it takes place in the venture, thus leading to a technology formulation that responds to market demand. While there is some debate about the need for a certain degree of technology push, there appears to be a broad agreement among authors of entrepreneurship and innovation that the balance needs to be tilted in favor of regular and significant input from the marketplace, that is, technology development as a need-based concept. Roberts[36] indicates that 60 to 80 percent of successful innovation projects in the United States and Great Britain were substantially developed on the basis of need definition, demand-pull influences. In their seminal study of electronics firms in post-war Great Britain, Burns and Stalker[37] reported that most firms in their research never matched their expertise at the technical level with equal investment and expertise in marketing and sales and subsequently floundered. They quote the example of radar development and how the key to its success and early deployment during the last war by Great Britain was realized by bringing the technical development people together with users at a very early stage. Therefore, a much more efficient feedback of operational requirements by the defense forces led to supremacy over the Germans, who, from a technological point of view, started at the same level of expertise but did not obtain feedback information on prototypes from the military users.

My experience in biomedical technology indicates that science based innovation can appear to be spectacular in its potential applications and can often dramatically attract the attention of major groups in society. Consider, for instance, the attention that research and innovation in the areas of ophthalmology and eye care have enjoyed not only in the media but also among the industrial biomedical and investment communities. Vast therapeutic markets have opened during the last decade for new ophthalmic drugs, new devices and procedures such as intra-ocular implants, as well as equally important cosmetic markets for contact lenses and the related contact lens cleaning solutions. Or, consider the field of medical diagnostics where technological developments and discoveries in recent times have not only helped in more efficient clinical treatment of patients but also offered potential new uses in a myriad of new food, water, and environmental testing applications. Many of these have not yet been specifically defined! The strategic position of the technology, when first commercialized, is now much more critical than in other nonscience-based or nontechnology-based innovations. This requires *speed in technology development, protection of industrial property* through patents or other methods, as

well as delineation of *early market positions.* All these activities are supposed
to take place while all the potential applications might not yet be known!

• Market feedback from potential users should be solicited as early as possible in
the technology assessment and development process.

• Review of potential applications of the technology that contrasts it against
the entire array of existing and imaginable uses is indicated.

Both these activities should be ongoing.

2.5   Organization in the Scientist-Started New Venture

This section deals with organizational design and structure considerations that are
unique to the scientist-started new business venture.   Here I will review
organization theories and literature dealing with organizational life cycles and
structure.

How does the history of its formation and the requirements of the new start-
up venture influence the organization? What organizational phases, or lifecycle
steps, can the venture expect to go through, and with which anticipated
implications?   What are the specific implications for the high-technology,
scientist-started enterprise? It should be recalled that this study deals primarily
with the pre-venture planning stage and the initial start-up phase when the
multitude of venture tasks are being organized. During these phases, all
preparations are made to arrive at a first marketing effort or, in the case of a
predominantly R&D company, to commence technology work on contracts or
in partnership with third parties. This section of chapter 2 reviews organization
theories that deal with lifecycle phases as well as forms of organization
structures and management processes in an effort to find answers to these
questions.

Organizational lifecycle theories have attempted to categorize the phases
through which an organization typically passes from planning and inception to
maturation and possibly dissolution. In these studies the various stages are
described, and the organizational tasks at each stage are linked with typical
aspects of management behavior during the same, previous, or subsequent
phases. It is then proposed that understanding all aspects of these typical phases
can assist in diagnosing and resolving related problems that could distract from

achieving desired conditions and performance. Three prominent works by Greiner, Adizes, and Burns and Stalker are considered here for the study of the scientist-started new business venture.

Adizes[38,39] divides the organizational lifecycle into the following phases:

- The Courtship Stage
- The Infant Organization
- The Go-Go Stage
- The Adolescent Organization
- The Prime Organization
- The Mature Organization
- The Aristocratic Organization
- The Early Bureaucracy
- Bureaucracy
- Death

Each of these phases is characterized in terms of four task orientations of the organization and its leaders. **PAEI** abbreviates these orientations as follows:

- **Produce:** for producing the desired results;
- **Administer:** sequence the timing and intensity of actions;
- **Entrepreneuring:** changes requiring creativity and risk taking;
- **Integration:** the team effort to coordinate missions and tasks.

The Integration activity is the one that is important in all lifecycle phases in order to build teams and create the necessary common understanding and commitment to corporate mission, strategy, and objectives, throughout the organization. The other three activities are required in varying degrees of intensity, depending on the lifecycle stage of the venture. In the Courtship Stage, Entrepreneuring dominates in the pre-establishment mode. The selling of the idea for the venture to others, to themselves, reinforces the necessary commitment to build a new business organization. The Infant Organization represents the venture, once established. Tasks move from Entrepreneurial to Producing. Funding is applied; few policies, procedures, or systems yet exist; the organization is in a *doing* mode. This is a highly centralized organization with entrepreneur(s) running the show. In the Go-Go Stage, with a working organization at hand, Entrepreneuring becomes the dominant activity. The focus is on how the Producing capable venture can exploit opportunities "out there." Signs of failure in this phase appear when the organization is unable to depersonalize itself, separate itself from the personalities of its founder(s), or institutionalize leadership and policies. In the Adolescent Organization, Administration arises as a dominant activity to enable the organization to cope with the higher volume and complexity of daily tasks. If increased allocation of resources to administration are made at the expense of attention to entre-preneuring, premature aging occurs, and the venture becomes short-term oriented. Some of the time that was spent selling and producing is now allocated to organizing. Particularly in this stage, a high risk exists for the formation of two camps--the entrepreneurially dominated and the administration-oriented groups.

The phases of the scientist-started new venture which are the subject of this study--pre-venture planning and initial venture operation--can coincide with Adizes' Courtship, Infant, Go-Go, and Adolescent stages. The major variants in our study from Adizes' model lie in the nature of the lead entrepreneur. As this role is filled by a scientist, neither entrepreneurial nor administrative roles might develop as projected in the Adizes model. Judging by published cases of scientists who became involved with venturing activities, it appears reasonable to assume that the scientist usually has no difficulties seeing himself as an entrepreneur, whether he has acquired helpful entrepreneurial skills or not. However, with reference to the earlier discussion of scientists' characteristics, I expect a low likelihood that the scientist-entrepreneur will anticipate and promote administrative tasks inside the organization when required. Whether or not the scientist-entrepreneur could be expected to play the role of an organi-zational integrator, remains an open question to which I see no systematic answers or even tendencies. Adizes' "Produce" covers not only technical development and production in the traditional sense but also other activities to produce the desired results for the firm such as marketing and selling. In a non-marketing fashion, the scientist-entrepreneur might identify with the producing role in that his orientation will be toward research and technology development activities.

My interpretation of the Adizes model suggests, particularly in the Go-Go and Adolescent stages, that scientist-started ventures tend to underemphasize the required marketing and administrative activities while, at the same time, no assurances exist that the Integrator role will be carried out as required. In order to assure market-defined or need-defined feedback and to continually support the product and scan for new applications and market segments, an appropriately sized and funded marketing, sales, and distribution component is just as important as the research, product development, quality control and technical services segments of the organization. The resource allocation, market segmentation, and prioritization issues that result are of strategic importance to the entire venture and are ideally resolved at the level of the multidisciplinary venture management team.

Greiner's[40] model of organization development identifies five dimensions to define this process.

- Age of the organization
- Size of the organization
- Stages of evolution
- Stages of revolution
- Industry growth rate

Against this framework, five phases of growth are identified in terms of dominant management styles and problems.

Phase 1: Creativity; the start of the enterprise by entrepreneurially and technically oriented founders preoccupied with making and selling products. As volume and complexity of activities increase, (unwanted) management responsibilities of an administrative nature increase. Leadership crisis occurs. A strong manager is required who masters business techniques to lead the organization.

Phase 2: Direction; a capable business manager installed, a functional structure is introduced as well as administrative and control systems. The manager and his direct team set the pace and direction, other levels are treated as functional specialties. This management style eventually becomes too centralized to effectively direct a larger, more complex organization. Lower level employees have insufficient latitude to carry out their role. The autonomy crisis occurs. Most companies now move to greater delegation.

Phase 3: Delegation; management by exception, delegation, creation of profit centers. Decentralization allows greater motivation, creativity, and market coverage. At some point in this phase autonomous actions in subgroups can lead to lack of coordination. The control crisis has arrived. Special coordination techniques are introduced.

Phase 4: Coordination; company units are merged into product groups, headquarters staff develops planning, reporting, and control procedures. These activities provide all company members with a view of total company objectives and procedures. Rewards focus on identification with corporate performance.

The red-tape crisis occurs as the headquarters-generated policies and procedures become bureaucratically overwhelming.

Phase 5: Collaboration; this phase leaves many procedures in place but emphasizes interpersonal collaboration. Problem solving through team approaches, reduced headquarters staff, matrix organization, team conferences, economic rewards focus on team efforts versus individual achievements. Greiner speculates that the next crisis might lie in the area of psychological saturation by the intensity of effort required of teamwork. To allow, within company cultures, for a reflective structure to stimulate perspective is offered as a possible solution.

Although it allows for the external dimension of the growth rate of the industry, Greiner's model is in large part based on the assumption that "the future of an organization may be less determined by outside forces than by the organization's history."[41] This led to a review of organizational growth phases from an organization's internal perspective. An understanding by management of these phases allows the use of company history to anticipate, in a timely fashion, the possibility of crisis and demands for change in organization, management processes, and orientation. In this process, management style is directly linked to management problems. The particular implication of Greiner's model for the scientist-started venture lies in the need for the scientist and his partners in enterprise to understand these organizational cycles and how founders' behaviors might impact them.

The Courtship Phase, The Infant Organization, and the Go-Go Stage of Adizes appear to overlap with the Creative Phase of Greiner in that they are heavily oriented toward entrepreneurial and production activities. The Adolescent Organization would coincide approximately with Greiner's Direction Phase in its growing emphasis on administrative activities. It would appear that because of its detail of identified activities in the various stages of the company lifecycle, Adizes' model can be of greater use in analyzing the specific implications for scientist-started new business ventures. From a philosophical perspective, Greiner's model contributes to our study by underlining the need for knowing, at any one time, precisely where the scientist-started venture is in the developmental sequence and which internal actions can be taken to enhance the venture's evolution.

Finally, we should discuss one of the original contributions to the theory of organization in the technological firm. "In their most general form, the findings of this research can be put into two statements: Technical progress and organization development are aspects of one and the same trend in human affairs; and the persons who work to make these processes actual are also their victims."[42] In the study of scientist-started and managed ventures this prophetic statement by Burns and Stalker can often be observed to be true in more than one way and on multiple occasions. Previously in this chapter, I referred to Burns and Stalker's The Management of Innovation in the context of scientists' characteristics and planning for technological ventures. The basic contribution of their research lies in the development of the organic and mechanistic organization models.

Organic Model

- definition of realistic individual tasks in terms of firm's common objectives,
- adjustment of tasks through communications,
- individual responsibilities not to limit initiatives and abilities,
- commitment to the firm, not to technical tasks only,
- chief executive is not omnipresent,
- communication is advice, not instruction oriented, and flows both horizontally and vertically,
- all functions, technical and nontechnical, contribute equally.

Mechanistic Model

- differentiation of individual functional abstract tasks without connection to common objectives,
- reconciliation of tasks through strong hierarchy,
- identification with hierarchy,
- total knowledge only at the top,
- communication is instruction oriented and flows vertically,
- local knowledge is more important than overall knowledge.

Based on their research, Burns and Stalker postulate that the developing technological organization tending toward the Organic model would be more successful in meeting its objectives. In such an organization, the firm would be better equipped to constantly optimize technological and marketing variables while simultaneously adjusting the internal organization to the external situation. The Organic model projects a fluid organization without boundaries to the demands placed on individuals and implicates all members in the concern's success. The Organic organization is a change organization. In placing emphasis on lateral communications, on the individual's role in overall success, and the equal importance of both technical and non-technical activities, it can nurture the start-up technology-based venture by providing the widest consideration and development of chosen alternatives of technological and marketing opportunities. The Mechanistic model represents the needs of a stable organi-zation beyond the initial phases of start-up, exploration and development.

When reading The Management of Innovation which was published in 1966, I was impressed with the timelessness of some of its descriptions and findings. Today, when the current needs of the innovation oriented enterprise are discussed, as, for instance by Moss Kanter,[43] emphasis is placed on the need to combine the individual entrepreneurial traits of the venture with the professional and disciplined aspects of the traditional corporate organization, a hybrid solution for which Burns and Stalker's Organic Model can be viewed as the forerunner.

Adizes' early stages of venture development--Infant Organization, Go-Go Stage, and the beginning of the Adolescent Phase--appear to coincide with Burns and Stalker's model of the Organic organization. The organization has not yet become fully administration oriented, certainly not evolved to any level of bureaucracy! Adizes' model, again, provides a more detailed categorization of the types of activities and developmental stages. However, the contribution of Burns and Stalker lies in specifically addressing the technological aspects of the developing firm.

From an organizational perspective, I have reviewed here the importance of the following issues in the scientist-started new business venture:

• depending on the particular stage in the venture, a need may exist for a different balance of entrepreneurial, production, administration and integration skills.

• recognition of the need for the Integrator role to be played in the venture to assure that all functional issues are pulled together and the team develops and maintains common goals.

• adoption, in the early venture stages, of a fluid, nonbureaucratic organization to optimize technological and marketing variables.

• awareness that the scientist-started venture may underestimate the importance of administrative and market-related activities.

• knowledge and awareness, at any time, of which stage of development the new venture represents, allowing pro-active management of anticipated challenges.

2.6   Summary, Conclusions and Propositions

In this chapter, I have elaborated on those theories and thought processes that could assist in the development of a theory of the scientist-started new business venture. In that process the subject was not only reviewed from the perspectives of management and organization, but also touched upon behavioral, anthropological, and sociological aspects. At the outset of this chapter, I stated that this study would be exploratory in nature. I have found relevant literature regarding the phenomenon studied in this book, but limited research dealing *specifically* with the scientist-turned-entrepreneur and his venture.

The summaries of each section were presented at the conclusion of each part of this chapter and do not need to be repeated here. Upon review, these issues all reflect a need for special attention in the light of the *potential for significant differences in cultural and behavioral backgrounds* which can be represented in the scientist-started venture. These issues appear to fall into a number of groups which are discussed below.

Training: The diverse backgrounds which would likely come together in a scientist-started venture would indicate that training is a major organizational need, for both scientists (in business and management skills) and for non-scientists (in technological fields). Such training would also assist in the development of common venture goals and cultures.

Technology Domination: In business and strategic planning, in building the organization and staffing the venture team, in defining the tasks and skills required and in resource allocation, scientist-started ventures will tend to become technology dominated at the expense of non-technical tasks.

Technology and Market Assessments: To translate the technological idea into a market opportunity demands thorough, comprehensive, and creative assessment exercises which, in turn, require planning and execution, sometimes needing skills not available within the venture.

Organization: A fluid, flat and non-bureaucratic organization in style and structure that addresses the entrepreneurial, production, administration, and integrative requirements of the venture at its various stages of development will allow identification of individual tasks and objectives with common venture goals, thereby benefiting organizational performance. Awareness of the potential pitfalls and opportunities of each stage in the life of the venture is indicated.

Finally, to conclude this chapter, I state one specific conclusion and four propositions to be tested in the empirical research to be reported in part II.

I concluded that there is sufficient knowledge about scientists' behavioral characteristics to use such information in planning for a scientist-started venture, particularly in the areas of staffing, organization, technology, and market management. This knowledge, which is grounded in generalized patterns of scientists' behavioral attitudes could allow the marking of potential pitfalls during the planning and management phases of the high-tech business venture.

Proposition 1
During the planning and initial venturing phase of the scientist-started business enterprise, technology will tend to be overemphasized as evidenced through functional patterns in staffing, organization structure, and resource allocation.

Proposition 2
The scientist who, in the formation and start-up phase of the enterprise, recognizes the cultural factor (i.e. his lack of organizaional skills and the behavioral differences between scientists and managers) will be more successful in attaining business performance objectives.

Proposition 3
Formal technological and market assessment activities to identify developmental needs and opportunities will improve the likelihood of early funding, effective technology development and market exploitation.

Proposition 4
An informal but clear organization in the early stages of the venture in order to allow for the balancing of entrepreneurial, productive, administrative, and integrative skill requirements, will create a climate conducive to attaining organizational performance objectives. Awareness of the potential pitfalls and opportunities of each stage in the life of the venture would be valuable.

This chapter has provided a theoretical framework for the empirical observations of some 22 scientist-started business ventures which are described in part II of this study. In referring to the selection of theories that could assist in the study of the variables influencing scientist-started business performance, I am aware that, due to the exploratory stage of scientific research in this area, this selection was equally exploratory. I stated in chapter 1 that one of the three main objectives of this study is to conduct empirical research among a number of scientist-started new business ventures. Through this field work we will further develop our understanding of the variables influencing organizational performance in scientist-started business ventures as well as test the applicability of the theories reviewed and propositions developed in this chapter.

Reference notes

1. Acs, Zoltan J. and Audretsch, David B. "Editors' Introduction."
   Small Business Economics , Vol. 1, No.1, 1989. p.1.
2. Dubinskas, Frank A. "The Culture Chasm: Scientists and Managers in Genetic-Engineering Firms." *Technology Review*, Vol. 88, 1985.
3. Paulin, William L., Coffey, Robert E. and Spaulding, Mark E. "Entrepreneurship Research: Methods and Directions." In: *Encyclopedia of Entrepreneurship* , edited by Kent, Calvin A., Sexton, Donald L., and Vesper, Karl H. Englewood Cliffs, New Jersey: Prentice-Hall,1982.
4. Ibid., p.364.
5. Roberts, Edward B. "What We've Learned: Managing Invention and Innovation." *Research-Technology Management*, Vol 31, Jan/Feb 1988.
6. Danielson, Lee Erle *Characteristics of Engineers and Scientists, Significant for Their Utilization and Motivation.* Ann Arbor, Michigan: Bureau of Industrial Relations, University of Michigan,1960.
7. Dubinskas, op cit.
8. Dubinskas, Frank A. "Janus Organisations." In: *Making Time, Ethnographies of High-Technology Organizations* , edited by Dubinskas, Frank A., Philadelphia: Temple University Press, 1988.
9. Sindermann, Carl J. *Winning the Games Scientists Play.* New York: Plenum Press,1982. p.274.
10. Burns, Tom and Stalker, G.M. *The Management of Innovation.* London: Tavistock Publications, 1966.
11. Roberts, Edward B. and Wainer, Herbert A. "Some Characteristics of Technical Entrepreneurs." *IEEE Transactions on Engineering Management*, Vol EM-18, no 3, August 1971.
12. Litvak, Allan Isaiah and Maule, Christopher J. "Some Characteristics of Successul Technical Entrepreneurs in Canada." *IEEE Transactions on Engineering Management*, Vol-EM 20, No 3, August 1973.
13. Timmons, Jeffry A., with Smollen, Leonard E. and Dingee, Alexander L.M.,Jr. *New Venture Creation, A Guide to Entrepreneurship* Homewood, Illinois: Irwin, 1985. p.28.

14. Bartunek, Jean M. and Betters-Reed, Bonita L. "The Stages of Organizational Creation." *American Journal of Community Psychology,*Vol 15,No.3,1987.
15. Martin, Michael J. C. *Managing Technological Innovation and Entrepreneurship.* Reston, Virginia: Reston Publishing Company, Inc., 1984.
16. Martin, ibid., p.275.
17. Timmons, Smollen and Dingee, op cit., p.8.
18. Martin, op cit., p.227.
19. Roberts, Edward B, "Influences on Innovation: Extrapolations to Biomedical Technology." In: *Biomedical Innovation*, edited by Roberts, Edward B., Levy, Robert I., Finkelstein, Stan N., Moskowitz, Jay and Sondik, Edward J. Cambridge, Massachusetts: The MIT Press, 1981.
20. Drucker, Peter F. *Innovation and Entrepreneurship: Practice and Principles.* New York: Harper & Row, 1985.
21. Litvak and Maule, op cit.
22. Sindermann, op cit., p.143.
23. Simon, Jane. "The New Breed." *New England Business*, October 20,1986.
24. Van Brunt, Jennifer "Executive Hiring Trends: Entrepreneurs and Managers." *Bio/Technology*, Vol 6, September 1988.
25. Deutsch, Claudia H. " Staying Alive in Biotech." *New York Times*, November 6,1988.
26. Moss Kanter, Rosabeth *When Giants Learn To Dance.* New York: Simon and Schuster,1989.
27. Timmons, Jeffry A. "New Venture Creation: Models and Methodologies." In: *Encyclopedia of Entrepreneurship*, edited by Kent, Calvin A., Sexton, Donald L. and Vesper, Karl H. Englewood Cliffs, New Jersey: Prentice-Hall, Inc.,1982.
28. Drucker, op cit.
29. Timmons, Smollen, and Dingee, op cit., p. 233-234.
30. Drucker, op cit.
31. Dubinskas, Frank A. "The Culture Chasm: Scientists and Managers in Genetic-Engineering Firms." *Technology Review*, Vol.88,May/June,1985.
32. Martin, op cit., p.294.
33. Timmons, Smollen and Dingee, op cit., p.29-30.
34. Skinner, Wickham. "Technology and the Manager." In: *Readings in the Management of Innonvation*, edited by Tushman, Michael and Moore, William, L. Marshfield, Massachusetts: Pitman Publishing Inc.,1982, p. 465.
35. Ibid, p. 474.
36. Roberts, op cit., p.56.
37. Burns and Stalker, op cit.

38. Adizes, Ichak. "Organizational Passages, Diagnosing and Treating Lifecycle Problems of Organizations." *Organizational Dynamics*, Summer 1979.
39. Adizes, Ichak. *How to Solve the Mismanagement Crisis*, Santa Monica, California: Adizes Institute,1979.
40. Greiner, Larry E. "Evolution and Revolution as Organizations Grow." *Harvard Business Review*, July-August 1972.
41. Greiner, ibid., p.38.
42. Burns and Stalker, op cit., p.19.
43. Moss Kanter, op cit.

Chapter 3

RESEARCH METHODS AND DESIGN

3.1 Introduction

The study of entrepreneurship is a multidisciplinary activity within the general domain of business administration and management research. Entrepreneurship research has surged during the last decade; however, it has been frequently anecdotal rather than systematic in nature. Little work has been done covering the venturing activities of scientists. To ensure a systematic approach to the study of scientist-started ventures and to make an initial identification of the variables involved, I planned and conducted (1) a literature survey and (2) an exploratory field survey . The review of relevant theories in chapter 2 identified a number of different areas of study that can be applied to the research of scientific entrepreneurship. Foremost among these is the area of management and organization as applied to entrepreneurial processes. This review also provided a framework for the organization of the case studies and their analysis. The overall goals of this study have been defined to include contributions to entrepreneurial research, as well as to have practical application for scientists, for the universities and research organizations with which they are associated, for potential management partners, and for venture capitalists. The research method and design used were adopted to reflect this multiplicity of purpose: to contribute to the entrepreneurial research base and to offer at least an initial insight to scientist-practitioners and their partners regarding this type of entrepreneurship, its challenges, and opportunities. The underlying principle has been to capture first-hand insights into the multitude of experiences of a number of scientist-entrepreneurs and their partners who have actually gone through this process. Experiences that qualify as *specific* to the scientific background of one of the partners are, of course, the main target of the investigation, particularly as seen from an organizational and entrepreneurial point of view. The study thus reviews the processes of technology generation and transfer as well as the planning, formation and management of the scientist-started venture with a view to identifying particular variables that influence organizational performance.

In planning the actual research methods and designs to be adopted in this study, I used the clear classification of Paulin, Coffey, and Spaulding in their chapter, "Entrepreneurship Research: Methods and Directions."[1] The authors divide this research process into five steps: (1) research purpose, (2) research strategy, (3) research design, (4) data collection, and (5) data analysis. My own research is primarily exploratory in purpose and uses ex post facto field studies as its approach. The research design is methodical, empirical, and comparative in nature. The research data collection relies on the use of personal, structured interviews, and the data analysis methodology is predominantly quali-tative.

In this chapter I will discuss the choice of research methods and designs and their application to the field study in detail. The remainder of the chapter is organized as follows:

3.2 Research Purpose
3.3 Research Strategy
3.4 Research Design
3.5 Data Collection
    3.5.1 The Interview Procedure
    3.5.2 The Interview Guide
3.6 Data Analysis
3.7 Boundaries of the Study

3.2 Research Purpose

The literature study, as described in chapter 2, confirmed the early assumption that little or no research had been undertaken in the entrepreneurial or management fields to investigate the specific aspect of *scientist-started* ventures. Some of the basic questions aimed at in this study were defined as follows:

• What motivates a scientist to cross over to the field of entrepreneurship?
• How do the scientists generally manage the dual relationships with their research institutions and ventures?
• How do scientist and team members arrive at a common venture culture and goals?
• How does the scientist select his partners?
• How does the scientist decide which role to play in the venture?
• What organization structures and reporting relationships are adopted?
• How does the scientist perceive the early planning and management phases of the venture?
• What are the scientists' and the team members' perceptions of the major driving and restraining forces associated with venture success?
• How do the relationships and variables that will be identified in answering these questions affect organizational performance?

In defining the formal ex post facto field study to approach these questions, I used my own experiences as well as input from the literature review. From the latter, I want to mention particular researchers who influenced this process. Dubinskas,[2] an anthroplogist at Temple University, who in mid-1980 was a visiting scholar at the Massachusetts Institute of Technology, contributed significantly to my understanding, from a *cultural* point of view, of the different worlds of scientists on the one hand and entrepreneurs on the other. Although many researchers have contributed to the field of innovation management, I was especially influenced by the works of E.B. Roberts at MIT who is one of the leading researchers in the area of *innovation and technology management* . Here I refer to Roberts' work in Biomedical Innovation[3] and throughout this book will reference a number of his other publications on innovation. Numerous works have been published recently on the various aspects of *entrepreneurship,* and I found New Venture Creation, A Guide To Entrepreneurship by Timmons, Smollen and Dingee[4] to be one of the most comprehensive, yet practical text- books. Still, the specific phenomenon of the scientist who endeavors to commercialize the technology himself, has not been the subject of thorough empirical work. Under the circumstances, I selected a research methodology that reflects the need to uncover the predominantly qualitative information about the venture planning and management processes embedded in opinions, procedures, and behaviors. This study is therefore primarily *exploratory* in purpose. It is intended to uncover and systematically describe presently unknown variables and their interrelationships. However, the study is not exclusively exploratory in nature. Research in the various entre-preneurial, innovation, organization and cultural areas, which are closely related to this subject, offer the possibility of defining a few initial hypotheses as a complement to this exploration. Therefore, the research purpose also includes a smaller explanatory component. *Exploratory research* is essentially inductive and descriptive and focuses on what phenomena occur and how. It uses descriptive, qualitative methods. *Explanatory research* ascertains and verifies causes and relationships between phenomena and is deductive in nature.[5]

3.3   Research Strategy

"The entrepreneurship literature contains quite a bit of informal, anecdotal theory developed from non-methodical research designs. About one-quarter of the studies on the entrepreneurship process were so classified. This type of work is valuable but can be difficult to evaluate or test empirically."[6] This quote from Paulin, Coffey, and Spaulding refers to their assessment of the research method-ology used in 81 entrepreneurial studies and can be interpreted as a general indication of the quality limitations of much of the early research work in this field. In recognition of my research purpose and to avoid these tendencies in previous entrepreneurial research, I developed the approach of a method-ological field survey using, in its design, the insights gained from a literature review as well as my own organizational and entrepreneurial experiences. As an approach to primarily exploratory research, the field study tool offers significant advantages over other approaches. "Field studies are strong in realism, significance, strength of variables, theory orientation and heuristic quality," writes Kerlinger[7.] Those apsects are precisely the ones demanded in the process of systematically identifying the phenomenon under study. The major weakness of this approach lies in its ex post facto character. However, the potential danger of this drawback can be minimized by instituting secondary data verification steps into the interview and data collection processes. Thus, in the exploratory mode of this research, I chose the ex post facto field study to identify the variables that occur in scientist-started ventures and influence their performance. Through the eyes and memories of the interviewees we learn about what happens in the process of starting and managing scientist-originated ventures. In addition, the study of case-related documents allows a further deepening of this exploratory understanding. This approach also lays the foundations for longitudinal studies in this area of entrepreneurship research.

3.4   Research Design

In its design this research was set up to be systematic and empirical. Inasmuch as scientists in both the United States and Canada were included, the research is also comparative. The point of departure in the research can be characterized by the question, "Which events are specific to the planning and start-up phases of ventures originated by scientists in the biomedical and related fields, and how do these events influence organizational performance?" To focus this question methodically, I used the following definitions to delineate the profiles of the scientist and his venture.

• **Scientist-entrepreneur**: the scientist whose primary occupation prior to playing a role in the venture start-up (and possibly concurrent with that process), was that of a clinician, researcher or teacher affiliated with a university, research institution, and/or hospital. Following the definition of the word *entrepreneur* described in chapter 2, the scientist in this study is thus involved in the processes of organizing, managing, and taking on the risk of a business. In this sense, the scientist leads or participates in an entrepreneurial management process whose objective it is to build a new business. This definition created the situational and time windows in which I had typically observed scientists' moves from the scientific to the entrepreneurial world and which was my basic motivation for undertaking this study. The industrial scientist-entrepreneur who, during his industrial affiliation, has usually been exposed to corporate and managerial cultures, is thus not included.

• **Scientist-started venture**: a biomedical business enterprise that was initiated or became commercially active during the last 12 years and in which a scientist, as defined above, played a key role in any or all of the planning, initial establishment or subsequent management phases. The period studied in the life of the venture typically covers from three to ten years but is primarily focused on the first three.

These definitions provided clear boundaries for the phenomenon to be studied in light of the questions enumerated above. I included both northeastern states of the United States and eastern provinces of Canada for two reasons. First, I wanted to search for variations in the findings based on country-comparative analysis. Second, this approach increased the geographical base from which we could solicit participation, without dramatically increasing time and budgetary demands which an all-United States or all-Canada study would pose. Although defined as an exploratory and qualitative study, I concluded that the study should cover at least 20 ventures to ensure an exploration of the widest variety of experiences in scientist-started ventures. To add to the systematic nature of this design, I set out to compile a listing of all ventures in the geographic areas described, which would potentially fit the two research definitions mentioned above. This list was partially based on ome published directories but was fleshed out with the help of the organizations listed in table 3-1. To verify with certainty whether the list included *all potential* participants was not possible. Published directories usually have a time lag of two to three years and will only include ventures that can be more easily identified. With respect to comparable knowledge in government and industry associations, we can be more confident. Most ventures, particularly ones that are science-based, apply for government grants or assistance at an early stage. The importance of networking for a start-up venture leads its partners to establish connections with industry associations.

Table 3-1. Sources of Potential Participant Listings

Mass.	Massachusetts Biotechnology Council	Industry Association
	MIT Entrepreneurship Forum	Massachusetts Institute of Technology
New Hampshire	Center for Venture Research	University of New Hampshire
	New Hampshire High Tech Council	Industry Association
Maine	Center for Venture Research	University of New Hampshire
Vermont	Office of Technology Transfer	University of Vermont
Quebec	Industry, Science & Technology Canada	Canadian Government
	Biotechnology Association of Canada	Industry Association
Ontario	Industry, Science & Technology Canada	Canadian Government
	Medical Device Association of Canada	Industry Association

The list generation effort resulted in a total of 47 potential ventures to be approached. All companies listed were approached by letter in February of 1989 with details of the study, and subsequently were followed up by telephone. Of these, 11 did not appear to meet the criteria of the definition of scientist-started ventures (see Table 3-3). The remaining potential base of 36 attracted 22 participants (a 61 percent participation rate). Table 3-2 shows the geographical distribution of the participants.

Table 3-2. Venture Participation

Massachusetts	7
New Hampshire	2
Maine	1
Vermont	4
Quebec	3
Ontario	<u>5</u>
	22

With respect to the period studied, two distinct time parameters were identified. First, the planning period covered the time between the actual technological development and the start of the venture. It was assumed that
understanding the pre-venture planning experience would be a beginning to
understanding the ensuing venture management period. The second sector studied
started at the time of inception of the venture. This study period covered the first
three years of the venture or ended earlier in case one of the following events
occurred :

• venture business failure or dissolution
• scientist's complete withdrawal from the venture
• venture sold

In other words, my objective was to understand and analyze the experiences
of 22 scientists through a comprehensive recounting of the scientist's
experiences and his evaluation of the planning and management processes within
his venture. To balance these observations, I also interviewed, in each case
study, a member of the venture's organization who was not the founding
scientist and who, by virtue of his position, had access to a full view of the
planning and management processes. Where available, annual reports, funding
prospectus, business plans, financial and funding data were also collected.

3.5   Data Collection

3.5.1   The Interview Procedure

The central data collection device chosen was the personal, structured interview.

The predominantly exploratory nature of this investigation dictated the need to be able to incorporate factual data collection as well as open-ended questions with the potential of yielding the widest array of answers and indications of variables and relationships.   To capitalize on the flexibility and potential wealth of data this design could yield, personal interviews, although time consuming, were essential. As a data collection tool, this method presented a number of additional attractions under these circumstances. Survey experience suggests that personal interviews provide a much greater participation rate than mail questionnaires. I projected a participation rate of 50 percent and achieved 61 percent. Reasons given for non-participation are shown in Table 3-3.

Table 3-3. Reasons for Nonparticipation

No time available to participate	8
Not willing to disclose any information	4
No response	2
Total ventures invited but declining to participate	14
No scientist involved in venture founding	7
Not a biomedical venture	4
Ventures not invited to participate	11

My experience during the last ten years in working with scientists in the biomedical field indicated that a defined block of time, without any need for prior preparation on the part of the scientist, could be an attractive survey procedure, perceived by the participant to be less time-consuming than completing a mail questionnaire. Following the initial letter with the project description, scientists were contacted by telephone, sometimes by fax, to discuss the project with them. Once scientists agreed to participate, they were asked to mail a copy of their resume as well as summary information on their venture such as business or product brochures, business plans, annual reports, or other publications. This allowed me to study the scientist and his company in general, prior to the interview. The scientist was also told that no preparation was required for the interview and that all identifiable data would be held in confidence. Subsequently, an interview time was set. The scientist was given the choice of time and location and virtually all participants chose to be interviewed at their primary place of work. On average, the interviews with the scientist took two hours and twenty minutes, with a range from a minimum of one and a quarter to a maximum of four hours. After the interview, the researcher chose which individual affiliated with the venture would be approached to participate in the nonscientist interview. This second interview was arranged and a separate trip undertaken for the interview. In a few cases, the second interview was carried out by telephone. This interview procedure was designed to assure the fullest independence in information gathered during the two interviews. The use of tape recorders has the advantage of literally recording the entire interview and the disadvantage of inhibiting participants to explore freely their experiences with the interviewer. I decided for two reasons to limit the process to note-taking. First, the anticipated length of the interview would have required tapes to be changed several times, thus again attracting attention to the device. Second, because the interview guide anticipated discussions of personal income as well as personal views of venture team conflicts and personalities, I judged the use of tape recording as potentially too inhibiting. I therefore chose an alternative whereby I made elaborate notes of key points during the discussions and then transcribed them in detail, usually within two days after the interview. Where required, I called the interviewee to clarify points after initial review. In addition to the actual conduct of each interview, a further two to four hours per interview was spent working out notes and observations on the interview instrument. A total of 42 interviews was conducted. The field study component of the research took place during the period of March through October of 1989.

3.5.2 The Interview Instrument

"We have been emphasizing that conceptual frameworks, research questions, and sampling matrices have a legitimate focusing and bounding role within a study. They give some direction to the researcher, prior to field work, by clarifying what he or she wants to find out, from whom, and why. Some direction is needed--but not too much; it is important not to foreclose on other ways of construing and addressing the main research issues that the fields site can disclose."[8] It is in this sense, as described by Miles and Huberman, that I approached the development of the interview instrument. An interview guide is typically made up of identification information, socioeconomic data, and, finally, those questions related to the problem. The detailed makeup of the schedule is discussed below. Other than in the identification and socioeconomic sections, I chose to use primarily open-ended questions to explore the participants' experiences. "Open-ended questions are those that supply a frame of reference for the respondent's answers, but put a minimum of restraint on the answers and their expression."[9] Kerlinger attributes additional advantages to this method such as the ability to allow probing, follow-up of unclear items, and evaluation of the respondents' true intentions and attitudes. This exploratory potential was reinforced by including a number of funnel type questions that start out being general and allow, with follow-up questions, a focusing on the respondents' range of experiences. In addition, the experiences were, in certain instances, ranked by the interviewees, expressing priorities and a sense of urgency as experienced in their process of planning and venture management. To minimize the disadvantages of the open-ended question (primarily loss of focus and objectivity) I followed the criteria of question-writing as treated by Kerlinger[10], as well as the more philosophical discussion of qualitative research instrumentation by Miles and Huberman[11]. The interview instrument was thus developed as a *flexible guide to conducting discussions* with the scientists as well as nonscientists. Although it is a standardized instrument, used in all interviews, the objective was for it to be applied loosely so as not to force the discussion in a direction that the participant did not want to take at the time. Generally, during the interviews, all questions were touched upon, although sometimes in a different sequence than the one suggested in the guide. The nature of the guide therefore allowed the widest possible angle to capture information from the interviewees, whether anticipated or not while, at the same time, providing a background structure. The latter assured that the general plan of questioning interviewees concerning the processes of technology development and transfer, venture planning, and management and organization processes was followed during both interviews. The establishment of a guide was also required in order to allow replication by other researchers and to establish the basis for longitudinal research.

The instrument received its pilot test in an interview with the first scientist in March 1989. Following this field test, a number of minor modifications and simplifications were introduced. The final version of the interview guide was used from the second interview onwards. During both the first and second interviews, I was joined by a business researcher from the University of Vermont who was present to provide a second, objective opinion on the performance of the instrument. The individual sections of this finalized document are further highlighted below.

- The first section covers basic venture and scientist data including socioeconomic background information. This section was always completed first. Since it does not include any potentially sensitive data, it also performed the function of permitting the scientist and the researcher to get acquainted.

- Section two deals with the scientist's <u>technology development and venture planning experience</u>. In addition to collecting a broad array of information about what was important and what tasks and skills were required in this phase, it selectively endeavors to let the scientist rank the importance of these tasks as well as describe his perspectives on playing an entrepreneurial role.

- In the third section, the emphasis is on evaluating the <u>post start-up venture management experience</u> and discovering what were the major driving and restraining forces influencing organizational performance in the perception of the scientist. This section further probes the organization structure and management processes adopted and records the scientist's perception of organizational success.

- Section four covers the <u>team member's background data</u> and motivation in joining the venture.

- Section five mirrors section three question-for-question and solicits the <u>team member's post start-up management experience</u> and so provides an alternative source of information on this process of early venture management.

- In the sixth and last section, <u>basic financial numbers</u> are solicited as well as the sequence of equity funding covering the first three years of the venture and the most recent year. This information will help to evaluate organizational performance from a quantitative perspective and compare it with the qualitative information collected in the interviews.

3.6   Data Analysis

In the design and implementation of a plan for the data analysis of these 22 ventures, I made use of <u>Qualitative Data Analysis, A Sourcebook of New Methods</u> by Miles and Huberman.[12] They have brought a systematic approach to the analysis of multiple site organizational studies. In traditional case analysis, particularly involving a large number of cases, the substantial volumes of narrative data collected can easily overwhelm the researcher and lead to the loss of thorough analysis and simplified or slanted conclusions. "There are usually so many contending dimensions, and so many alternate realizations to these dimen-sions, that it is easy for researchers to lose intellectual control, get overwhelmed with the multiple possibilities and finally say, 'There's no rational way to do this.' Setting up the possibilities in matrix form helps."[13] Miles and Huberman present an array of matrices and displays that can be used to condense qualitative information and make it accessible in compact forms. This process is made up of data reduction and data display. Several cycles or iterations of this process will systematically make the original data more transparent and allow juxtaposition of data to explore and discover hidden relationships. Conclusion drawing and verification is an integral part of these iterations. This process needs to be documented not only as a control on the analytical process but also as documentation of the learning process itself, as the following chapters show.

3.7 Boundaries of the Study

The strength and validity of the research methods described in this chapter are subject to a number of limitations.

Ex post facto field studies identify and analyze variables through the eyes and memories of their participants. This introduces the danger of loss of objectivity. The design of the interview instrument and procedures was arranged so as to minimize such bias. First, the questions were formulated to avoid pressure on the interviewee that any particular line of answering might be more desirable than another. Second, some questions in the guide were repeated in a modified sense to obtain a second answer to the same question. Third, most of the questions asked of the scientists were also asked of the venture team member, thus establishing a second point of view. In the fourth place, the researcher--not the scientists-- chose the second person to be interviewed in each case. Finally, documentation and financials regarding the venture were sought to review the congruency of answers provided and complete a full "picture" of each venture. Of course, while the attempt was made to minimize bias, it cannot be completely excluded.

In addition, there is the question of the representativeness of the sample of these field studies. There can be no certainty that the list of potential scientist-started new ventures did, as attempted, represent all such ventures or even a very significant portion thereof. In fact, it is probable that despite my thorough search in the states and provinces, even with the help that was obtained from government and industry association organizations, this only led to an approximation of a list of all potential ventures that fit the research definition. Furthermore, those ventures which were identified but which decided not to participate, whatever their reasons, withheld their experiences from this study. In this manner, there could be limitations and biases introduced to the input into this study and thus to its conclusions. However, as indicated earlier in this chapter, the research approach is primarily exploratory in nature, providing a potentially wide array of variables describing the phenomenon, with its validity therefore, not critically dependent on principles of statistical significance.

Finally, in this type of social research, there is a built-in propensity to study successful or, at least, surviving organizations. The cause of this is related to the fact that failing or failed ventures are rarely systematically identified by such organizations as governmental agencies, industry associations, or directory publishers. The latter usually work with a two-year to three-year publication delay. In entrepreneurship publicity and even research, the successful ventures usually attract more attention than the failures and nonperformers. During the period of this study, three of the twenty-two participating ventures closed down and one or two more struggle on with basic viability questions. While I accept this bias away from the study of failure, it also needs to be noted that the very study of venture planning and management processes, deals specifically with the foundations and variables of future venture organization performance. The exploratory nature of the study allows us to identify an array of potential variables of venture success and failure for future study.

Reference notes

1. Paulin, William L., Coffey, Robert E. and Spaulding, Mark E. "Entrepreneurship Research: Methods and Directions." In: *Encyclopedia of Entrepreneurship*, edited by Kent, Calvin A, Sexton, Donald L. and Vesper, Karl H. Englewood Cliffs, New Jersey: Prentice-Hall,Inc., 1982.
2. Dubinskas, Frank A. "The Culture Chasm: Scientists and Managers in Genetic-Engineering Firms." *Technology Review*, Vol 88, May/June 1985.
3. Roberts, Edward B. "Influences on Innovation: Extrapolations to Biomedical Technology." In: *Biomedical Innovation*, edited by Roberts, Edward B., Levy, Robert I., Finkelstein, Stan N., Moskowitz, Jay and Sondik, Edward J. Cambridge, Massachusetts: The MIT Press, 1981.
4. Timmons, Jeffry A. with Smollen, Leonard E. and Dingee, Alexander L.M.,Jr. *New Venture Creation, A Guide to Entrepreneurship*. Homewood, Illinois: Richard D. Irwin, 1985.
5. Paulin et al., op cit., p.354.
6. Ibid., p.357.
7. Kerlinger, Fred N. *Foundations of Behavioral Research* , New York: Holt Rinehart and Winston, Inc.,1973, p. 406.

8. Miles, Matthew B. and Huberman, Michael A., *Qualitative Data Analysis.* Beverly Hills: Sage Publications,1984, p. 42.
9. Kerlinger, op cit., p. 484.
10. Ibid., p. 481-489.
11. Miles and Huberman, op cit., p. 42-48.
12. Miles and Huberman, ibid.
13. Miles and Huberman, ibid., p. 42.

Part II

Scientists as Entrepreneurs

Chapter 4

SOCIOECONOMIC PROFILES OF THE RESEARCH PARTICIPANTS

4.1 Introduction

Part I defined this study in terms of existing literature and applicable theories, as well as its empirical research methodology and design. Part II examines the field studies among scientist-started new ventures in detail. These field studies were specifically designed with the primary objective of observing the planning, entrepreneurial, and early management processes in such scientist-started firms and chapter 5 reports on these findings. Yet the study also yielded significant additional data not directly related to these processes, touching upon socio-economic factors and such other aspects as technology transfer, university relationships, and comparative management issues.

The purpose of this chapter is to review the socioeconomic data collected concerning the scientists and their ventures. Our starting place in the field research was a given group of scientists and ventures that resulted from the selection and participation procedures described in the previous chapter. The study conducted a *qualitative* analysis of how scientists fared in the organizational and management processes of the initial venture stages. Thus, the primary emphasis has not been on a quantitative analysis of background characteristics; however, socioeconomic data was collected in defining the research participants. Where appropriate, these data are compared with published research on entrepreneurs in the United States and Canada. This data also contributes to the specific exploratory thrust of the research.

Although the specific participating scientists and ventures are, with their approval, identified by name, the case data contained in the remainder of this book has, at the request of a significant portion of the participants, been reported in a coded or otherwise anonymous fashion so as to maintain confidentiality. This chapter is organized into four additional sections.

4.2   Scientists and Ventures
4.3   Some Characteristics of Scientist-Entrepreneurs
4.4   Venture Profiles
4.5   Summary

4.2   Scientists and Ventures

In chapter 3, I described the methodology employed in identifying the potential ventures that would be asked to participate in the research project, as well as the process of obtaining the approval of the scientists and their business partners involved to carry out this study.   There was only one case in which the participants were reluctant to be identified as founders of the venture. A more prevalent concern was expressed about the possibility of being publicly and individually quoted. While the motivations behind this reluctance were not systematically researched, my conclusion in this respect is that in most of these cases the participants preferred not to be seen as restarting discussions about previous conflicts or troublesome management experiences with partners, managers, universities, or other third parties.

Table 4-1 identifies the participating scientists and their ventures. The heading "Scientific Affiliation" relates to the university or research institution with which the scientist is connected, or with which he was affiliated prior to and/or during the initial stages of the venture formation. At the time of this study eight of the originating scientists remained active (full time) with these universities, and in chapter 6 I will elaborate on the various aspects of scientist -university relationships during and following venture creation. Eight of the ventures in the study are located in Canada (CAN) and the remaining fourteen in the United States (USA).

Table 4-1. Participating Scientists and Ventures

Participating Scientist	Venture	Scientific Affiliation
Thomas G. Adelman, Ph.D.	ImmuCell Corporation, US	University of Southern Maine
Francesco Bellini, Ph.D.	IAF Biochem International, Inc. CAN	Institute Armand Frappier, Universite de Quebec
Henry E. Blair	Genzyme Corporation, US	Tufts University
David K. Boraker,Ph.D.	Chromogen, Inc.	University of Vermont
Theodore E. Cadell, Ph.D.	CME Telemetrix, CAN	University of Waterloo
Stanley E. Charm, Sc.D.	Penicillin Assays, Inc., US	Tufts University
Robert C. Dean, Jr., Ph.D.	Verax Corporation, US	Dartmouth College
David S. Dime, Ph.D.	Toronto Research Chemicals, CAN	University of Toronto
Nathan B. Dinces, Ph.D.*	Medarex, Inc., US	Dartmouth College
Robert J. Emerson, Ph.D.	Shelburne Laboratories, Inc., US	University of Vermont
Horace W. Furomoto, Ph.D.	Candela Laser Corporation, US	Avco Everett Research Labs - NASA
Walter Gilbert, Ph.D.	Biogen, Inc., US	Harvard University
Barry W. Glickman, Ph.D.	Probtec Corporation, CAN	York University
Serge Gracovetsky, Ph.D.	Spinex Medical Technologies, CAN	Concordia University
Robert Heft, Ph.D.	IBEX Ltd.,CAN	M.I.T.
Philip M. Lintilhac, Ph.D.	Liveco Biomechanical Instruments, US	University of Vermont
J. A. Lowden, M.D., Ph.D.	HSC Research Development Corp., CAN	Hospital for Sick Children University of Toronto
Kenneth G. Mann, Ph.D.	Haematologic Technologies, Inc. US	University of Vermont
Perry Rosenthal, M.D.	Polymer Technology Corporation, US	Harvard University
David A. Swann, Ph.D.	MedChem Products, Inc., US	Harvard University
Robert B. Salter, M.D.** & John Saringer, P.Eng.***	Toronto Medical Corporation, CAN	Hospital for Sick Children University of Toronto
Chamer Wei, Ph.D.	Transgenic Sciences, Inc., US	Tufts University

* Represented the founding scientists
**No formal ties with the venture but a supporter and the originator of its technology
*** Founder-scientist-president

4.3   Some Characteristics of Scientist-Entrepreneurs

This section provides additional insight into the family background of the scientist-entrepreneur and reviews selected venture statistics. A number of studies of entrepreneurship have been conducted on the background characteristics of entrepreneurs in general and of technical entrepreneurs in particular. These research efforts cover demographics such as age, family background, education, and country of origin.

In comparing the statistics of this research with previously published studies in Canada and the United States, I particularly relied on the works of Litvak and Maule,[1] Roberts and Wainer,[2] and Roberts and Peters.[3] In the following tables, the current research is discussed and compared with trends shown in these earlier studies.

In recording the age at which scientists became involved with the new venture, I referred to the year in which the venture was first firmly structured, that is, when some basic funding was obtained, one or more employees were operational and the venture had generally passed through the basement or garage stages of early development. This adjustment to the date of venture inception was only applicable to three ventures which had been intermittently committed to or were dormant before being restarted. In those cases the restart dates were used. The rationale for taking this approach lies in the realization that the full commitment of the scientist to move ahead with the venture, financially and career-wise, took place at that later date. One of the reasons quoted frequently for the particular time chosen for the establishment of the venture is related to a perceived unresolved or unsatisfactory relationship with the scientific institution with which the scientist was affiliated. Chapter 6 will address these concerns in further detail.

Table 4-2 shows the age distribution of the participating scientists at the time of venture inception. The mean age of the scientist in this sample is 43, and 57% of the scientists fell into the 41 to 50 age range. This is at variance with the age range found by Litvak and Maule[4] who reported that technical entrepreneurs in Canada and the US typically started their ventures in the 35 to 40 age range. I believe that two explanations could be evaluated in accounting for this difference. First, the career differences between technical entrepreneurs and scientist-entrepreneurs should be considered. Members of the latter group were observed to be settled into the relatively secure worlds of academics and research, and it commonly appeared to take an extended period for scientists to decide to fully or partially step out of that world and into the entrepreneurial environment. The second reason for the higher age range would likely be the additional years expended by scientists, in comparison with the overall population of technical entrepreneurs, in completing their university education. 91% of the scientist-entrepreneurs in the studied population had completed doctorate degrees. For only two of the twenty-two scientist-entrepreneurs was the current venture not the first one they had started. Therefore, for most of the participants the higher age could not be explained by the time spent on developing prior companies.

Table 4-2. Age of Scientist-Entrepreneur at Venture Start

Age Group	Total	Canada	USA
26-30	1	1	-
31-35	3	2	1
36-40	3	1	2
41-45	6	2	4
46-50	5	1	4
51-55	3	1	2
	21	8	13
Age Range	29-54	29-54	35-54
Mean Age	43	40	44
Median Age	44	43	45

Data on the founding scientists in one participating company was not disclosed and therefore the socioeconomic tables in this chapter only report on 21 scientists. In chapters 5 and 6 this firm *is* represented through the participation of another scienstist who is also affiliated with that venture.

In "Some Characteristics of Technical Entrepreneurs," Roberts and Wainer[5] developed and provided empirical support for a model which proposed that the entrepreneurial orientation of an individual is originally derived from family back-ground and further influenced by education, goal orientation and motivation. Figure 4-1 highlights these relationships.

Figure 4-1.
Model of Factors Influencing The Development of an Entrepreneur

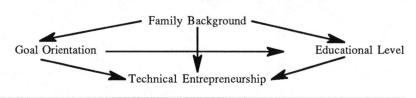

from: Roberts and Wainer, "Some Characteristics of Technical Entrepreneurs" 1971

Goal orientation and motivation of the scientist are discussed in detail in the following chapter which deals with the entrepreneurial and management processes of the scientist-started new venture. In the area of education, Roberts and Wainer in their American study, and Litvak and Maule in their Canadian study of technical entrepreneurs both noted the high levels of education of such entrepreneurs relative to the general public. Of these entrepreneurs, 86% (US) and 59% (Canada) held university degrees. This level of education could be expected with technical entrepreneurs where technical training and experience are forces drawing these persons toward technology-based entrepreneurship. In my study, education levels were even more pronounced, with all scientists having completed university education and 91% holding doctorate degrees.

Particularly noteworthy with respect to family background are the findings that fathers who were self-employed, and thus involved in entrepreneurial activities, were more likely to raise children who would eventually become entrepreneurs than were nonentrepreneurial fathers. Both Roberts and Wainer and, Roberts and Peters conducted original research in this area. This phenomenon is attributed to the demonstration effect that the father's occupational activities have on his children; it can also be observed in other career fields. Roberts and Peters explain it as follows: "It seems quite likely, therefore, that any relationship between entrepreneurship and a family background in which the father was self-employed is due to the son's familiarity with the conditions of self-employment and the possible association found in other studies between need for independence by a father and his sons."[6] Roberts and Wainer found that the entrepreneurs in their study were more likely to have self-employed or entrepreneurial fathers than would be normally expected based on U.S. Census data for the entire population. In fact, 50% of the entrepreneurs in that study had entrepreneurial fathers versus 24% in the overall population. Litvak and Maule reported 39% self-employed fathers in their study of Canadian technical entrepreneurs. Table 4-3 shows that these trends could also be observed in the present research, with 48% of the total number of scientist-entrepreneurs reporting that their fathers were self-employed.

Table 4-3. Father's Occupational Status

Status	Total	Canada	USA
Self-employed	10 (48%)	4	6
Employed	11 (52%)	4	7
Total	21 (100%)	8	13

Of particular interest in the area of family background is the finding by Roberts and Peters that idea-exploiters, that is, scientist-inventors who took steps toward exploitation of their inventions, were most likely to be firstborn sons.[7] In fact, 96% of the strongly exploited ideas among the MIT faculty studied were those of scientists and engineers who were first born sons.

To start to explain the phenomenon of birth order, I will use a quote by William D. Altus from his in-depth review of research studies in this area. "In my opinion, the most prominent of the presumed social causes' is likely to be the differential parental treatment accorded children of different ordinal positions, to greater 'conscience' development, greater dependence on adult norms and higher expectations of achievement falling to the lot of the firstborn."[8] Altus shows, for instance, a higher than chance occurrence of firstborns among graduate students. By being both scientists and entrepreneurs, participants in this research could be expected to show a high rate of firstborns among them relative to the general population. Table 4-4 confirms this trend with respect to the scientist-entrepreneurs.

Table 4-4. Firstborn Status

	Total	Canada	USA
Firstborn sons	17 (81%)	8	9
Not firstborn sons	4 (19%)	0	4
n=21			

Immigrants to Canada and the United States have been motivated to move to their new countries because of greater economic opportunities and social freedoms. In pursuit of these objectives this group and their children have produced a greater than average number of entrepreneurs relative to the general populations of these countries. In Litvak and Maule's study of technical entrepreneurs, 38% of the entrepreneurs were immigrants who came to Canada to improve their economic well-being and provide better opportunities for their children. Table 4-5 similarly shows a high ratio of immigrants among the scientist-entrepreneurs studied.

Table 4-5. Country of Origin Status

	Total	Canada	USA
Immigrants	7 (33%)	3	4
Non-immigrants	14 (67%)	5	9
n=21			

4.4   Venture Profiles

In this section, a profile of the ventures will be defined in terms of ownership, age, number of employees, and selected financial data.

In 91% of the start-up enterprises the scientist-entrepreneur had an equity stake from inception. Of the two scientists who had no equity, one had founded the company on behalf of a clinical and research institution, and the other had an agreement that a portion of the shares would be assigned to him once the venture was taken public as planned. At the time of this study, the percentage of scientist-shareholders had dropped to 82% due to the fact that two scientist-entrepreneurs had sold their stakes in the corresponding ventures. Thus, in terms of putting their own resources at risk, the majority of scientists in this study truly became entrepreneurs! Between the founding of the enterprise and the time of this study, the scientist's equity share typically fell due to dilution caused by additional outside financing or the addition of new partners. This was the case in 13 ventures. In only two cases did the equity share of the scientist go up during the same period through additional capital contributions by the scientists. In three ventures, all fully or majority controlled by the scientists, equity shares stayed at the same level from inception of the company up to the time of this study.

Table 4-6 provides an insight into the age and size of the ventures in this research project. For this purpose, I chose the number of employees as an indicator of company size because this was the only data readily available for all 22 participants. As in the overall population of start-up companies, the size of the scientist-started ventures tended to increase with venture age, although not at a predictable rate. This unpredictability is rooted in the fact that science-based companies, when funded only to do further technological development work (as opposed to also commercializing products or services), grow slowly in their early stages in terms of employees and revenues.

The age of these companies was rather evenly distributed with a mean of six years. During the first four years of operations, the ventures typically remained relatively small and employed up to 20 people. In subsequent years, employment growth accelerated and in ten years commonly evolved to more than 100 employees. Public companies were in existence longer and had more substantial numbers of employees than privately held firms.

Table 4-6. Venture Age and the Number of Employees in 1989

Venture age in years	Ventures in this age range		Number of employees in these ventures, respectively		
	number	%			
1 - 2	4	(18.2)	5,6,9,14	mean:	9
3 - 4	6	(27.3)	3,5,8,12,25,70	mean:	21
5 - 6	2	(9.0)	13,97	mean:	55
7 - 8	5	(22.7)	8,20,24,35,72	mean:	32
9 - 10	1	(4.5)	450	mean:	450
11 and up	4	(18.2)	50,165,230,258	mean:	176
	22	(100.0)			

Notes:
mean venture age: 6 years   mean number of employees: 72
venture age range: 2-12 years   employee range: 3-450

publicly held firms: mean venture age 7.6   public: mean number of employees: 13
privately held: mean venture age 5.0   private: mean number of employees: 3

Developing a generalized financial profile of the typical scientist-started venture was a more complex task. Initially, 20 of the ventures were funded with private money. Two firms had gone public concurrently with the inception of the firm, the remaining six completed public offerings within three to five years from their startup date. Raising public money at venture inception is a rather rare phenomenon because it requires highly advanced, proprietary technology and substantial scientific affiliations. Thus, at the time of this study, eight of the ventures (or 36%), were publicly financed. Fourteen of the participants (64%) were privately held.

In only three instances was the scientist the sole or majority provider of the initial start-up funding. At the time of this study the same three companies.were still exclusively funded by insiders, that is, founders and working partners. However, it was most common for multiple funding parties to be involved, either as partners or employees or both, or as outsiders.

Half of the privately financed ventures did not make a complete set of financial and funding data available to this research but most of these did indicate whether their firms were profitable or not. The remaining seven only provided financials on a confidential basis. Together with the publicly traded companies, the study therefore collected financial information on 15 ventures. Table 4-7 provides an array of financial information to define the ventures without disclosing individual company data.

Note that the average age of the publicly traded firms at 7.6 years was fifty percent higher than that of *all* the companies that were privately held (mean age 5.0 years) and more than twice as high as that of those privately companies which disclosed their financials (mean age 3.3 years). The difference in average annual sales was even more pronounced with public companies at $11.3 million versus privately held at $.5 million. Since their inception, the public companies had typically raised substantially larger amounts of money in more frequent financing rounds. On average, these companies raised $7 million per funding drive for every $2 million obtained by private ventures.

The profitable firms, both the public and private ones, showed age and sales figures *at or above* the mean age and sales numbers for their respective group. This trend was most pronounced in sales of the public companies. I concluded that, *given* that certain organizational and management conditions are achieved, profitability is more likely to occur in older firms which have already risen to a larger size. Organizational performance will be further discussed in chapter 5.

It is interesting to note that the difference between private or public ownership appeared to have little influence on the scientist's continuing involvement in the venture or on its profitability in the year of the study. In approximately half the ventures, in both privately and publicly held firms, and irrespective of whether they worked full time or part time at these companies, the scientists were still in control at the time of the study in such roles as chief executive officer or chairman of the board. An additional 40% remained involved in the venture, though not in a chief executive position. Approximately one-quarter of the companies reported being profitable.

Table 4-7. Venture Funding, Sales, and Profitability*

Funding Source	Number of Ventures	Mean Sales** ($ 000)	Mean Venture Age(yrs)	Number of Ventures Profitable	Avg. Number of Funding Rounds
Public	8	11,258	7.6	2 (25%)	4
Private	7	516	3.3	2 (29%)	2.7
Total	15***	6,789	5.6	4 (27%)	3.7

* Financial data relate to the latest year available at time of study; fiscal 1988, 1989
** Annual sales numbers in US $; converted Canadian $ @ .85 US $
***Fifteen ventures reporting financial data

These exploratory investigations lead me to the hypothesis that revenues in public companies grew at a faster pace than in the private ventures because of the former's access to greater financial resources and the fact that these public firms had been in operation longer. The sample size on which these financial data are based is small and for more definitive answers about the differences between privately and publicly financed scientist-started ventures, additional research would be required.

4.5 Summary

The mean age of scientist-entrepreneurs at the time of venture inception was 43 and this was found to be higher than the 35 to 40 years reported in other studies. The longer education required to complete doctorate degrees (91% of the scientist entrepreneurs possessed Ph.D.'s), and the extended periods that scientists often took to commit to entrepreneurial activities outside their universities, would explain these age differences.

In terms of family background, 48% of the scientist-entrepreneurs had self-employed fathers and 81% of them were first-born sons, confirming previously reported tendencies on these questions. Following previously established data, a relatively high proportion (33%) of the scientist-entrepreneurs were immigrants.

The mean age of the participating ventures was six years. The number of employees ranged from 3 to 450 with a mean of 72. Typically, through the first four years of operations, employment grew to around twenty people and reached one hundred employees before the tenth year.

The majority of the scientists (60%) were found to remain in some form of controlling position with their ventures through the time of the study. This trend was present among privately and publicly held firms. Full-time or part-time status with the company did not appear to be a variable influencing a scientist's continued involvement.

Scientist-entrepreneurs, in addition to restructuring their careers, put their own resources at risk in their ventures, although their equity share dropped as the firm went through successive funding drives.

At the time of the study, eight (36%) of the ventures were publicly held and fourteen (64%) remained privately financed. The public companies had a mean age of 7.6 years and the privately held firms a mean age of 5 years. The average sales for the public companies was $11.2 million per year at the time of the study. For the seven private companies who did disclose their financials, a much smaller average annual sales number of $.5 million resulted. Funding availability to promote accelerated growth of the venture and the longer period during which public companies had operated were considered the key reasons for this substantial difference in turnover rates.

This review of the socioeconomic parameters of the scientist-entrepreneur and his venture gives greater definition to the participants in the study. Although the number of participants was limited, the data appeared to confirm trends previously established in related research projects.

Reference notes

1. Litvak, Isaiah Allan and Maule, Christopher J. "Some Characteristics of Successful Technical Entrepreneurs in Canada." *IEEE Transactions On Engineering Management*, Vol. EM-20, No.3, August 1973.
2. Roberts, Edward B. and Wainer, Herbert A. "Some Characteristics of Technical Entrepreneurs." *IEEE Transactions On Engineering Management*, Vol. EM-18, No.3, August 1971.
3. Roberts, Edward B. and Peters, Donald H. "Commercial Innovation From University Faculty." *Research Policy*, No. 10, 1981.
4. Litvak and Maule, op cit.
5. Roberts and Wainer, op cit.
6. Roberts and Peters, op cit., p.119.
7. Ibid.
8. Altus, William D. "Birth Order and Its Sequelae." *Science* , Vol.151, January 7,1966, p. 48.

Chapter 5

PLANNING AND MANAGEMENT IN SCIENTIST-STARTED VENTURES

5.1 Introduction

This chapter will investigate why scientists decide to play a role in commercialization activities, how they plan for their ventures, and, finally, how their enterprises are managed in practice. I have further divided these questions into a number of detailed areas that were covered in the field research. After describing the experiences observed in each area, each section will finish with some interpretative and concluding comments.

To start this exploration we review how the scientist-entrepreneur was defined in chapter 3. "The scientist whose primary occupation, prior to playing a role in the venture start-up, and possibly concurrent with that process, was that of a clinician, researcher, or teacher affiliated with a university, research institution and/or hospital." Whereas the term *entrepreneur* is sometimes used to describe primarily the lead entrepreneur, the definition of *scientist-entrepreneur* used here implies only that the scientist plays a role in the organizational, managing and risk-taking processes. The scientist is thus not only a manager, he clearly puts at risk his own resources, such as money, time and position at the research institution. He is thus involved in what Drucker[1] has called the *entrepreneurial management process*.

For the purpose of this study, organizational performance is described as the manner and degree to which entrepreneurial and management processes contribute to the achievement of organizational objectives of the enterprise. Organizational performance is measured by studying functional and integrative processes devised in order to meet these objectives. The title of this book Scientists as Entrepreneurs: Organizational Performance in Scientist-started New Ventures, is to be understood in the context of these definitions.

In this exploration, I occasionally let the scientists and their team members speak for themselves through the use of tables which summarize their experiences and opinions systematically, before moving on to interpretation and conclusions. This approach allows the reader access to both the summarized but uninterpreted empirical data and to the author's evaluation of the findings.

This chapter is further organized as follows:

5.2   The Scientist's Commercial Vision
5.3   Why Play a Role in the Venture? Which Role Was Played?
5.4   Business Training and Experience of Scientists
5.5   Scientists' Perspectives on Venture Tasks and Required Skills
5.6   Venture Team Formation
5.7   Funding and Timing of the Venture Start
5.8   Technology and Market Assessment
5.9   The Initial Venture Organization and Management Processes
5.10 Driving and Restraining Forces Shaping Venture Success
5.11 Evaluation of Venture Performance
5.12 Scientific and Business Cultures
5.13 Summary
5.14 Conclusions

5.2   The Scientist's Commercial Vision

In chapter 2 the scientist was defined as "one learned in science and especially natural science; a scientific investigator", and technology was "applied science; a scientific method of achieving a practical purpose." When and how does such a scientific investigator extend his scientific explorations to include not only a technological but also a commercial vision? Through which phases can the scientist typically be expected to have to travel? Figure 5-1 illustrates a simplified sequence of events of what might logically be expected to happen from scientific investigation to commercialization.

Figure 5-1. From Scientific Investigation to Commercialization

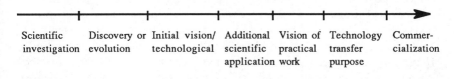

Scientific investigation	Discovery or evolution	Initial vision/ technological	Additional scientific application work	Vision of practical purpose	Technology transfer	Commercialization

In each case some of these events could take place concurrently or in a different sequence. To achieve an improved understanding of the scientist's motivations in reaching for personal entrepreneurial and management experiences, the field studies also investigated the period prior to commercialization and venture start.

In the ventures studied, as in my own experience, almost all scientists who arrive at a practical if not outright commercial vision do so based on their own particular area of scientific investigation and expertise. Occasionally, one encounters a scientist who in his pursuits has moved from one scientific area to another, sometimes to quite an unrelated area of study. In such cases the scientist has typically treated the new area in the same way any unfamiliar field is usually approached by scientists--primarily through scientific self study!

The pursuit of a certain area of science does not automatically lead the scientist to decide to participate in its commercialization. Two conditions need to be satisfied. First, the scientist should recognize the opportunities for the practical applications of his science. Second, the scientist must consciously decide to become active outside the scientific realm. The latter decision will be reviewed in a later section; here the development of the applied vision is examined further.

Chapter 6 will explore the issue of technology transfer, from the scientist with a commercial vision in a university environment to implementation in a new company. The broader question of "How does a scientist move beyond the pursuit of knowledge to develop ideas about the application of his science?" is beyond the scope of this study. Nonetheless, some insights were gained during the conduct of the field research. Three-quarters of the scientists reported that they themselves generated the initial vision for a practical or commercial

application of their scientific work. In half of these cases this practical vision
appeared to be the direct result of the scientist's own extrapolation of the
potential capabilities of his discovery or development. In the other half, this
discovery of the practical potential was facilitated or accelerated when the
scientist juxtaposed his scientific work against an external situation. For
instance, such situations as contacts with a technology transfer director at a
university or research institution, or with a company, or through an event such
as a direct exposure to a perceived market need, would allow the possibility of
bringing the science and its application together in the mind of the scientist.
The remaining quarter of the scientists interviewed, reported that *outsiders
directly* provided the first idea for a commercial application. Thus, a minority
of the scientists reported having *independently* created the commercial idea for
their venture; it more commonly took outside influences to move from scientific
development to commercial vision. This is not so surprising when considered in
the light of Dubinskas' observations regarding cultural differences between
scientists and businessmen. "Scientists see the goal of producing scientific
knowledge as primary, and they tend to devalue economic goals in their world
view. There is an aesthetics to this appraisal, too, where open-ended scientific
work is more pleasing or 'elegant' than the accomplishments of business ends
motivated by short-run goals."[2] In order to "see" the applied and commercial
opportunities, the scientist must consciously or unconsciously decide to go
outside the realm of the pursuit of scientific knowledge!

5.3 Why Play a Role in the Venture? Which Role Was Played?

What, indeed, motivates a scientist in the biomedical and related sciences to
attempt to play a role in an entrepreneurial activity? Why does the scientist, in
addition to, and even in competition with, an often tenured position at a
university or research institution, aim his sights at a commercial venture? To
begin to understand the various perspectives involved, Table 5-1 lets the
scientists themselves speak to these questions. Note that the 22 cases have been
coded A to V and this coding is held constant for the remainder of the book.

There appears, at first sight, to be a wide variety of motivations and roles
manifested by the scientists. Closer examination allows certain tendencies to
emerge. With respect to the question of why the scientists decided to play an
entrepreneurial role, the answers varied from making money as the most important perspective, to a singular need to advance scientific and clinical objectives
through the technology in question.

Table 5-1. Why Play a Role in the Venture?

Scientist's Perspective	Which Role Played?
A Create a scientist-run company to apply science; be an entrepreneur, run a business.	Represented all involved scientists; carrier of the vision and drive, the catalyst.
B Only way to spend his career in this science area; be a successful entrepreneur, build a business.	The key scientist.
C Pursue scientific objectives and application; stay with it, build a successful business	Scientist-inventor-technologist
D A unique scientific opportunity; be an entrepreneur, make money, build a business.	Synthesis of unrelated scientific areas brought into the venture.
E Make money, put a company together, a thrill; pursuit of clinical and scientific work.	Understanding of the technology and contrast this with market demands and opportunities.
F Application of science, putting scientific ideas into action; make money.	External role: establishing research and commercial relationships.
G Use successful science background to build a successful business; apply science to the market.	The traditional leadership role.
H Be both a successful scientist and businessman; science a prime motive.	Catalyst for team building and science orientation.
I Become a businessman, make money.	Manager and lead scientist.
J Freedom from university or corporate rules; build successful firm; fun to work at; money.	Troubleshooter, team facilitator.

K	Build an applied scientific company; personal achievement; investment opportunity.	Provides overall direction, major investor.
L	Scientific opportunity for societal good; contribute to building a company; equity.	Catalyst in forming and running the company.
M	Scientific achievement prime consideration; keep business quite separate from science.	Glue that holds it all together.
N	Develop what is scientifically possible; company with total independence; success in business as in science; make money.	Invented products; organized and managed the company.
O	Scientific/clinical perspective; need to achieve and succeed; make money.	Define product performance, market vision; build team, make decisions.
P	Science is the dominant objective; form company only to get research funding.	Makes all final decisions.
Q	Build successful business; make money.	Venture is scientist's idea & creation
R	Scientific & clinical perspective; personal achievement, build a business.	No company w/o his leadership; he hurts company by not effectively dealing with people.
S	Scientific/clinical perspective; no fees or equity.	Advisor w/o pay or equity from the start.
T	Building a business; achievement; mading money.	Knows the technology; knows customer needs.
U	Scientific freedom to pursue vision; business to focus science; personal achievement, income.	Mostly as creator of science.
V	Personal achievement, wanted to build a successful company; make technology work.	Critical in identifying market opportunities; in R&D program; in building venture team.

With respect to the monetary perspective, one scientist stated during the interview: "I don't know what other scientists have told you, but I will not hide the fact that becoming an entrepreneur and the potential to make money, as I saw was possible, attracted me. Maybe they feel it too, but just don't admit to it." Indeed, many of the scientists listed the opportunity to make money as one of the important motivations to play a role in a new enterprise, yet only one participant expressed it as the most important consideration.

The more prevalent perspectives, both in terms of importance and frequency, related to seeing the enterprise as an opportunity to advance scientific objectives and vision, and to build a successful business as a matter of personal achievement. Within these two latter themes are many variations, as can be seen from the summary in table 5-1. There is, for example, the scientist who for many years has supported a venture based on his technology with free advice and without any expense reimbursements, or equity position. His motivation has been to support the development of the medical equipment in question in order to help in the widespread clinical application of his discoveries. At the same time he has found it incompatible with his position as a scientist and clinician to have a financial motivation at stake, and he has left the commercialization effort to a scientist-engineer from his university. Still another scientist has used a new venture solely to provide funding for his research, which he could not have otherwise obtained. These two examples are exceptions to the motivational patterns that this study discerned. The important feature of what was observed lies in the multiplicity of perspectives quoted. The majority of the scientists reported to be motivated by a combination of reasons, the three most important ones being listed in table 5-2.

Table 5-2. Scientists' Key Motivations in Entrepreneurship

Advancement of science and its application	19
Personal opportunity to build a business, become an entrepreneur or businessman	18
Opportunity to build equity, make money	12
n=22	

Table 5-1 also reports on each of the roles the scientists described in the planning and development of the venture. Although, at the time of this study, 14 of the 22 scientists carried out full-time duties in connection with their ventures, I concluded that the distinction between full- or part-time commitment could not be used to characterize the role the scientist played in the entrepreneurial and management processes. Indeed, some full-time scientists adhere to work schedules that allow them to maintain full-time positions at both their universities and ventures. Some full-time scientists no longer connected with a university direct the venture's research in all its aspects, or direct the entire venture in the role of president or CEO. Others act on a strictly part-time basis as chief scientific officers or as chairman of the board. The influence the scientist has over the venture does not appear to relate to the amount of time he spends with it.

In order to study the roles the scientists played in these ventures, I return to the organizational lifecycle model of Adizes[3] which was described in chapter 2. Each of Adizes' lifecycle phases is described in terms of the following four task orientations, abbreviated by **PAEI**:

P = Produce: producing the desired results;
A = Administer: sequence the timing and intensity of actions;
E = Entrepreneuring: changes requiring creativity and risk taking;
I = Integration: the team effort to coordinate missions and tasks.

I concluded in chapter 2 that, on the basis of their scientific objectives and activities, and their need to build businesses, the scientists typically played Entrepreneuring and/or Producing roles. Based on the field studies, my assessment of the scientists' roles in their ventures is that all of them played Producing roles in generating and supporting the required science and technology: whether full-time or part-time; whether they focused on technology only or were involved in general management issues as well; whether they had invested personal monies in the ventures or not. In their contribution to the venture's vision and in their drive and activity to support the startup process, 21 of the 22 scientists also played Entrepreneuring, that is, creative and risk-taking roles, though in varying degrees of intensity. As expected, none of the scientists was seen to play a dominant or supporting role Administering. It was commonly anticipated by them that financial, administrative, and personnel related issues would, on a day-to-day basis, be carried by team members other than the scientist.

One-third of the scientists could be said to have played Integration roles in the venture. The Integration role is the one that keeps the company and its management team focused on the total mission by developing and supporting team formation as well as its identification with the enterprise's plans and visions. This Integration role is an important one which needs to be effectively covered during all stages of the company's lifecycle. Later in this chapter, I will address the issue of lack of Integration activity in the venture team.

Table 5-3. **PAIE** Roles Played by Scientists

Produce	22
Administer	0
Entrepreneuring	21
Integration	7
n=22	

At this point, I note that the motivations of the scientists in joining or starting a venture closely matched the roles which they subsequently chose to play in these new enterprises. The drive to build a successful business and make money, and the desire to develop the science and enhance its application coincide with the Entrepreneuring and Productive role definitions. These motivations and roles were widely observed during this study.

5.4 Business Training and Business Experience of Scientists

Earlier in the chapter I explored that point along the continuum from "science to sale" where the scientist had started to imagine the commercial application possibilities of a scientific principle or development. Furthermore, he has decided to play a role in the entrepreneurial process that lies ahead. In chapter 6 the subject of technology transfer will be considered in further detail. Suffice it here to note that in this research only four of the scientists considered outright sale or licensing of the technology involved, but decided against that alternative for one or more of the reasons discussed. There now exists a technological concept-- some idea about a practical opportunity for application of this concept; a scientist willing to invest time and other resources, and possibly a potential partner. In this and the following two sections, I will revisit the scientists and their partners as they begin to identify venture tasks and skills in preparation for the new firm.

Two of the participating scientists had significant and relevant previous business experience while also functioning as researchers in a university context. The remaining participants had not been involved in business operations, although another four had occasionally engaged in scientific consulting for companies. This finding could be anticipated in view of the definition of "scientist" which was employed and which tended to exclude all scientists who were not connected in some way, at least in the period prior to the creation of the venture, to a university or research institution.

In the section on the venture team in chapter 2, a number of authors were reviewed who have published studies concerning scientists and technologists in venture teams. The conclusions derived from this literature point to the absence of business training among such members. What is more, those who do identify a need for development of such skills will not usually carry through with the training they find desirable.

The present study confirms this noted tendency. Although five scientists had specifically considered this need in view of their entrepreneurial plans, none had implemented such training considerations. Thus, of the participants, none had actually pursued any formal business training activities such as courses or workshops. Lack of time was often cited as the reason. Typically, one scientist-entrepreneur reported that "there is no time to educate any of the venture partners in management skills." When this question is analyzed in detail, interesting further nuances appear. Four participants had approached this problem by self study, in the same manner that they would alleviate any other lack of knowledge in their scientific endeavors. However, this approach was not marked with success as they still mentioned selected business skills which they should be equipped with in order to be more effective in their venture roles. Half of the scientists actually discussed one or more specific functional skills which, after some time in the venture, they found themselves to be fundamentally lacking. Of those, *team management* and *interpersonal skills* were the most frequently mentioned omissions, followed by *inadequate funding* and *financial and marketing skills*. If we consider the cumulative impact of both scientists with these concerns and those who considered business training at the outset, over one-half of the scientists either implicitly or explicitly recognized a need for business training.

It was often postulated by the interviewees that the selection of the members of the venture team should ideally reflect a balancing of the skills required in view of the venture tasks at hand. This might then compensate for the skill deficiencies of individual team members, while safeguarding that the venture team possessed all the required talents. This study, however, consistently found a significant discrepancy between the recognized need for business skills on the part of the scientists and the action necessary to address this need.

Table 5-4. Scientists' Prior Business Training and Experience

Event	Yes	No
Has the scientist completed any formal business training?		22
Has the scientist considered business training at the beginning of the planning stage?	5	
Has the scientist experienced a lack of business skills since starting the venture?	11	
Has the scientist had previous business experience?	2	20

n=22

The literature and field studies surveyed here indicate that among aspiring scientist-entrepreneurs there is a considerable degree of recognition of the need for training in basic business and management skills. It is particularly noteworthy that the skills most frequently reported lacking were in the areas of team and people management. The inherent contradiction in this finding is that nothing was done to address this reported need. I submit three explanations for consideration.

1. It is in line with the generalized characteristics of scientists, as described in chapter 2, to learn skills by reading about unknown areas. The need for basic business training might be recognized, but the decision will be to read rather than to engage actively in practical training programs.

2. Several of the authors mentioned in chapter 2 have suggested that the scientists and technologists will be inclined to put technology above all other considerations in terms of what will make the venture succeed. Thus, even if the need is recognized and if skills are actually missed in the day-to-day running of the venture, the tendency will remain to stay focused on the

technology and undertake learning primarily in these areas.

3. Finally--and this explanation is not unique to scientist-entrepreneurs but applies to all start-up situations--consider the priorities in a new venture. In the planning and start-up phases, the emphasis will be on completing a myriad of tasks: technology assessment, business plan development, funding, facilities, market research, attracting partners. In this setting a rather more "reflective" activity such as learning skills, regardless of whether the need is recognized, will attract a low priority in comparison with all the urgent "doing" activities required of the entrepreneur!

Although each of these considerations suggests possible explanations for the discrepancies between the reported business training needs and what was done about them, an unexplained duality remains. It could be that active business learning is regarded as too abstract when the need for business skills is *first* realized, while in retrospect, the scientist still sees these skills, whether he mastered them or not, as a key to successfully executing the venture tasks at hand. Apparently, the benefits of active engagement in business studies, especially early in the venture, are not obvious enough to motivate the scientist to implement such training. Maybe this reluctance is related to the scientist's residual resistance to the business culture and the values it represents.

During the field studies, a few scientists and team members mentioned the need for business partners to acquire a basic, sound understanding of the technologies involved. Not only does this improve the business partner's ability to commercialize the technology, but such training also appears to increase the partner's ability to communicate effectively with his scientist regarding the technology-based venture and its success.

5.5   Scientists' Perception of Venture Tasks

Which venture tasks did scientists perceive as necessary prior to the actual start of the enterprise? What is the relative priority of the tasks mentioned? The objective of this part of the study was to explore, through the eyes of the scientists, what needed to be done once they decided to involve themselves in the new enterprise. Understanding this phase of the venture's development also assists in an enhanced appreciation of the criteria employed for the selection of partners and team members. Table 5-5 summarizes the discussions with the scientists regarding the originally defined venture tasks and their priorities.

Table 5-5. Scientists' Original Perception of Venture Tasks

| Venture Tasks | Number of scientists mentioning item   (n = 22) | | |
	High priority	Low priority	All priorities
Further R&D	12	8	20
Financing & funding	12	4	16
Technology scale-up	9	7	16
Technical team formation	6	9	15
Facilities	8	6	14
Business & strategic plan	5	3	8
Venture management team formation	3	1	4
Marketing	2	1	3
Administration	-	-	-
Development of management skills	1	1	2
Other tasks	1	-	1
TOTAL	59	40	99

scale 1 through 6: high priority = top three ranked tasks;
low priority = bottom three ranked tasks

If all technology-related issues such as research & development, technology scale-up, technical team formation and facilities are considered together, they make up two-thirds of all the tasks mentioned by the scientists. Approaching the commercialization process of a science-based development from the scientist's viewpoint provides (as in the case of training requirements) a picture of technology focus and domination. From that perspective, it is understandable that the need for technical team formation is still valued more highly than that of venture management team development. The only nontechnological task that really competes for the scientist's attention is financing and funding.

In any venture, funding takes on a major importance because it is perceieved as critical by all partners of the venture, irrespective of their functional roles. In the entrepreneurship literature, as in these field studies (and I underscore this through my own experiences), funding becomes the issue which embodies the different values and visions of the scientist versus those of his business partners! Funding determines such pivotal elements as the date the venture can start, the possibility of acquiring research or production equipment, the budget for serious marketing work, the first paychecks after working out of basements, garages, or makeshift laboratories. In short, it symbolizes the key to the opportunity! For the scientist there is an additional and important reason to recognize funding often and with a high priority, as confirmed in this investigation. Funding and financial issues are often where the different behavioral and cultural backgrounds of scientists and businessmen meet or clash! Funding and the need for a return on investment exemplifies the often-cited (by scientists) shorter term and goal-oriented focus of the businessman and the entrepreneur. This is in contrast with the wider purpose of the quest for knowledge and the longer time frame in which scientists tend to express their visions.

It could, of course, also be stated that the importance of the funding task can hardly be overvalued and that the process by which funding is acquired is often not adequately understood or addressed. Successful entrepreneurs, whatever their backgrounds, expend time, attention, and thoroughness in developing a key variable in funding: the business plan. "How important is a business plan? Without it, raising venture capital or other formal or informal financing is nearly impossible--unless, of course, you don't need it." Timmons' statement here is unequivocal.[4]

Venturing scientists' lack of recognition of entrepreneurship and management as serious disciplines would also explain the low importance attributed by them to the tasks of business and strategic planning and administration. It should be pointed out, however, that there was no relationship found between the eight scientists who originally recognized business planning as a high priority venture task and the organizational performance of their ventures. Section 5.12 will further discuss the issue of how the different business and scientific cultures interact and what can be suggested to improve the effectiveness of venture management teams based on such radically different backgrounds.

5.6 Venture Team Formation

From the evaluation of tasks required in the venture start-up and the skills which the founders believed they could personally bring to these enterprises, the study moved on to the way the venture team evolved. How did the scientist choose his partner(s)? What kind of people did the scientist look for as partners or team members? Which criteria were commonly used to select these people? Once again, to provide a full view of the reported experiences in this area, I let the scientists who participated in this exploratory study express themselves. Table 5-6 provides a synopsis of each scientist's early experience in venture team formation.

Table 5-6. Initial Venture Team Development

Scientist's Views of This Process (n=22)

A. Venture originated by venture capitalists and scientists; none as full-time .partners. A group of scientists directed R&D. First hired scientist to head laboratory; then COO, lawyer and accountant from the corporate world. Primarily functional hiring criteria. "A scientist-run company."

B. Venture started by two scientist-friends: one full-time from inception, the other full-time when venture could support it. Financing and marketing skills obtained by educating themselves; no senior business people hired during first seven years. Only functional hiring criteria emphasized.

C. Venture started by the scientist in his spare time. Educated himself about business by developing university courses in business and teaching them; hired engineering skills. After many years concluded he needed a professional businessman as partner to lead him and the venture, and to manage the team.

D. Scientist is the sole entrepreneur, full-time; acquired funding and market skills himself; initial access to scientific and technological skills met through consultants. Hired scientific employees and administrator. Scientist reports not being motivated to deal with administration!

E. Scientist and his entrepreneur partner, both full-time. Primarily considered functional skills; saw the need for a professional manager early on. Looked for executives who could see the connection between science and the market's needs. CEO hired two years after inception.

F. Scientist-entrepreneur, part-time, originally defined the administrative and technological skills required; filled openings with university associates whom he had long known. No professional business types yet hired; scientists took advice from board members and others.

G. Scientist initiated enterprise, full-time; hiring based on functional skills primarily. R&D director and financial director hired upon formation; technology transfer and sales directors two years later. Although prior business experience, scientist-CEO expressed his perceived lack of marketing and financial skills.

H. Scientist, with company backing, became full-time businessman in setting up biotechnology venture under his direction; only technological staff hired so far, scientist learned to administer.

I. Scientist-entrepreneur-CEO, full-time, instrumental in setting up biotechnology company. Looked for personality, nonbureaucratic, young people; also looked for functional skills and hired finance, legal, corporate development and manufacturing executives upon inception.

J. Two scientist-friends, full-time, started biotechnology firm. Considered skills and team fit with team; did not hire business professionals until three years after start. Then they took in business partner-CEO.

K. Scientist-entrepreneur, part-time, set up bio-instrumentation company. Important to have the right chemistry among team members; trustworthy, tolerant of scientists & functional skills. Businessman brought in six month after start.

L. Scientists (part-time), university and corporate partner set up venture. Corporate partner took care of all nontechnical tasks untill that partner pulled out!

M. Scientist and venture capitalists started company. Scientist did not want to be involved with full-time management; hired functional skills including R&D, manufacturing, COO soon after start of company.

N. Science-dominated venture set up by scientist, initially part-time. All other skills essentially "grown" in-house, market research and sales included; tried "professional" management from the outside, did not work due to lack of technological understanding or motivation of manager. Firm is seen as a family!

O. Scientists and an entrepreneur started firm, all on part-time basis initially. Profound emphasis on entrepreneurial team work and spirit; additional functional skills initially hired on a consultancy basis.

P. Scientists, venture capital firm, and university started venture. Hired professional manager strictly on the basis functional skills; business contacts, regulatory, fundraising, marketing experiences and exposure to bio-tech. Initial business work done by scientists; one full time, one part time.

Q. Scientist (full time) conceived of venture idea, took silent partners. Initially scientist did all tasks; general manager hired one year later. Relationships not designed to work as synchronized team.

R. Scientist originated venture, no business partners; carried out all tasks himself, full time. Hired and fired many employees; now recognizes need for people management skills. First professional manager hired 4 years after venture start.

S. Scientist-engineer started venture, full time, with financial partner and reports that, unfortunately, team fit and personality were not looked for in hiring. Lack of professional business skills; still run by founder. Professional manager joined as partner and has since left.

T. Scientist initiated firm. Full-time scientist did all jobs, hired only tech people, and admits he lacks people skills and underhired in the commercial area; professional manager joined four years after start-up.

U. Started by a scientist and an entrepreneur who had previously worked together, both full time. CEO-businessman joined upon inception; looked for team spirit, chemistry with team, sense of urgency, and functional skills. Only added ...financial controller plus a number of technology people.

V. Scientist started, full time, initially without partners. Added business and engineering partners, people he worked with before. Developed marketing ideas himself; made list of skills and team members, employees, and consultants needed. Interplay between business and science; neither was dominant.

A number of themes appear in this summary which were previously identified. Some of the scientists mentioned that they familiarized themselves with certain functional business skills and carried out some business-related duties themselves, rather than hiring others to do so. Again, the lack of functional business and people management skills is already noted at the initial stage by a small number of the participants. New notions that resulted from this part of the field research center on the kinds of criteria by which team members are selected and the timing of bringing professional managers on board.

More than half of the scientists indicated specifically that the only or primary criterion for hiring team members was defined in specific functional business skills. It is not known how many additional scientists used the same limited, functional criteria but did not mention this specifically during the interview. I believe there could have been a number of additional cases. Some of the scientist-entrepreneurs even made specific references to regretting this early hiring strategy. Scientists who did not start their ventures by themselves attached at least some importance to knowing their partners in advance. Somtimes, these partners were friends or colleagues with whom they had worked in previous situations. Thus, they learned to act as a team more easily because they already had much in common, both on a business and a personal basis.

During the fieldwork, I noted that few of the participants mentioned any selection criteria for personal characteristics such as fit within the team, personality, and so on, although the relevant question distinctly included the mentioning of both functional and personality attributes. In fact, only five scientists mentioned chemistry within the team as a significant criterion for evaluating candidates. The majority hired people for the venture on the basis of functional skills only. My interpretation of these trends is that they derive from the absence of a professional approach to organization and team building in these ventures, particularly in the early start-up phase. Both in the management and entrepreneurial literature, the importance of team fit and chemistry is strongly emphasized. It followed from the various interviews that the lack of emphasis on this issue had eventually contributed to a number of team or personnel management problems in these ventures. Half of the ventures reported serious venture team-related upheavals since inception, conflicts which are further explained in Table 5-11.

The second notion evolving from this part of the research dovetails with the first. The majority of the scientist-initiated businesses did not bring professional management on board until a later stage in the venture, varying from six months to ten years after inception. Team building and management skills, as well as other business skills, that might have been required during the early period, were thus not available.

In summary, these findings underline the trends described earlier in this study: namely, technological dominance, insufficient business, lack of management training and lack of an appreciation of team dynamics issues. This is not to imply that a scientist-entrepreneur cannot successfully lead his enterprise; indeed there are a number of capable performers among the participants. Rather, the likelihood of serious organizational problems, especially operational ones occurring in the early stages, is increased when the scientist himself or a partner or the team as a whole does not display the talents to resolve such situations. In the terminology of Adizes,[5] this problem is defined as a lack of Producing (in this case functional business) skills and a lack of Integration (in this case, people and team management) skills.

The study did not find any demonstrated lack of available venture partners as a reason for the absence of skills in the ventures. Team members who participated in the study gave three reasons for their initial attraction to the opportunity: (1) the basic potential of the technology as seen in the light of market opportunities; (2) the attractions of being involved with a promising ground-floor opportunity, including personal income; and (3) the relationship with the founding scientist and identification with his goals.

5.7 Funding and Timing of the Venture Start

So far this chapter has focused heavily on planning activities that predominantly occur prior to the actual start-up of the new firm. I say "predominantly" because many of the questions and issues discussed, such as team development and skill requirements, continue to play a role in all phases of the young company. The topics of the initial funding and the timing of the venture formation now move the study into the post-planning and start-up phase.

Scientists often created a bridging period in which their ongoing personal income requirements were being met, in part or in full, by their research institutions and, in a few cases, by their technological consulting practices. Most full-time academic and research situations appeared to allow for some time to be spent by the scientist on outside interests. In a few cases this time allowance was formally defined as 20 percent. Even when these arrangements allowed the scientist to put free time into his venture, funds were still needed for other purposes in order to start the firms. This bridging period, to which many scientists had, nevertheless put them at an advantage compared with many other groups of scientists in terms of income security. Table 5-7 identifies the major sources of initial funding. Initial funding is defined as the specific funds, equity or loans, in cash or in assets, that allowed the firm to open its doors at a given date and commence operations.

Table 5-7. Sources of Initial Funding

Included scientists' own funds	17
of which, exclusively scientists' funds	4
Other sources of funds	
Venture capital	3
University	3
Initial public offering	2
Government grants	5
Partners' money	10
n=22	

The scientists' financial commitment and involvement in the venture is underscored by the fact that three-quarters of them reported investing their own funds initially to enable the enterprise to take off. In the remaining ventures, initial funding had been organized through venture capital, initial public offering, loans and venture partners' monies, or a combination thereof. Of the other sources of funding, individual partners' money is the dominant one. Next to scientists' funding, partners were the most prevalent source of start-up capital. This result was somewhat different than expected. I had anticipated that the scientist would typically consider the technology and his time as the major contributions to the venture and would expect partners to put up the bulk of the funding. In later stages of these ventures the incidence of scientists who personally added funding was significantly lower. The study identified only five such instances.

The high incidence of scientists' investment at inception can be understood in two complementary ways. First, at the planning stage, when there is not yet an ongoing concern, scientists have not yet been intensively exposed to the business and financial worlds and the opportunities they see for outside funding are less prevalent. Basement, garage or laboratory located work on the technology is, under these circumstances, most easily funded by scientists' money, when available, and that of any early partners. Also, scientists might not yet be prepared to share or disclose their technology, as required by outside sources of funding. Second, in the post start-up phase, the money-raising ability of the venture can be expected to have improved as technology and business plans have moved forward and business partners have exposed the ideas to a larger population of potential funding sources.

Although government or other grants constituted only a small source of funding at inception, in later stages this source of funding was pursued and used more frequently. Government funding, subject to the governmental peer review and budgetary approval processes, was found to be appealing in the sense that it does not introduce into the young venture any outside interests or business pressures. The decision to limit funding to personal and grant sources has been cited regularly. Throughout the field studies a clear tension was observed between the desire to retain independence, often at the expense of limiting funding on the one hand, and the availability of adequate funds to develop the vision, on the other. No consistent pattern could be discerned concerning the way in which scientist-started ventures resolved these issues. However, over time and as dilution of the ownership occurred through venture capital participation and initial public offerings, this dilemma became less prevalent.

Table 5-8. The Critical Determinant in Venture Starting Dates

When funding became available	13
Change in relationship with university	3
Other reasons	6
n=22	

Funding and the starting date of the venture could logically be expected to be related. In this study, as can be seen in Table 5-8, that expectation is confirmed. The change in their relationships with the university concerned those scientists who concluded that they could not pursue technological and academic career visions any further within the confines of their research or academic institutions. The remaining reasons for the timing chosen ranged from the availability of a needed scientist to join the venture to a breakup with a scientific partner.

5.8   Technology and Market Assessment

The issue of scientific and technological domination in the activities of the young scientist-originated company has appeared throughout this study. One of my objectives in the fieldwork was to qualify this subject in further detail.

How does the scientist act to have his technology, the basis for the venture, accepted and reviewed in support of his commercial ideas? This question covers both the development of the technology in the venture as well as such aspects as independent scientific review, use of technological consultancies, and the establishments of boards of scientific advisors. Does understanding market applications for this technology, indeed, take a lower priority than developing the technology? Or, to put it in another way, does the scientist-started venture separate the scientific from the other activities required in completing the innovation loop?   E. B. Roberts'[6] definition, "innovation = invention + exploitation" includes the technological development as well as the delivery of this development to the practical application. In this sense, market research and marketing constitute aspects of the same technological innovative process.

Table 5-9. Initial Technology and Market Assessment

Technological assessment completed	16
Formal board of scientific advisors	3
Market assessment completed	5
Formal marketing advisors	0
n=22	

The technological and scientific review process is often a natural extension of the original work done by the scientist. In the research world, peer review and outside consultations are accepted procedures in checking validity and progress, and in obtaining the required inputs into the development processes. Even after the scientist had started his venture, he would often continue this practice as demonstrated in Table 5-9. In addition, a number of ventures were reported as being subjected to peer review in their applications for Small Business Innovative Research Grants from the National Institutes of Health or other federal agencies in the United States or National Research Council Grants from the federal government in Canada.

Few ventures formally established Boards of Scientific Advisors at the outset. Even ones that formed such boards at a later date attributed little direct
scientific or technological input to these groups but saw them rather as effective
means to manage the external scientific and business relationships of the company.

Five of the ventures reported having completed market assessments at the
time of venture start. In four of these, the scientists reported that, irrespective of
funding modes, they believed from the start that a viable venture would need a
thorough market assessment from the time of inception and that they supported
such research. A consistent pattern cannot be established from the study data as
to why companies would instigate this early process, or, as was mostly the case,
why *not* to carry out such evaluations at all or to delay them. The insights
obtained do provide, however, some possible relationships between the type of
venture and the likelihood of early market assessment. With two exceptions
where the scientists initiated market research, ventures that saw themselves
primarily as research and development companies in the early phase of venture development did not do market research work at that time. Companies that raised
capital at or soon after inception through initial public offerings had completed
formal market assessments and plans as part of the business planning exercise
that precedes public funding. The same could not be observed among companies
initiated by venture capital firms. These ventures delayed formal plans until a
later date and obtained the initial funding commitments based on overall
perceptions of commercial potential and, often, the reputation of the involved
scientists and their university ties.

Although the use of marketing consultants at this stage was not reported, a
few ventures obtained advice from board members or through other informal
means. In contrasting technology assessment with the early use of market
research and plans, this study provides, once more, insights into the dominance
of science and technology in venture planning and start-up.

5.9 The Initial Venture Organization and Management Processes

In this part of the study, the exploratory nature of the research emphasized the
observation of organizational and management aspects with a view to finding
those which might be particular to the scientist-involved nature of the enterprise.

To develop such insights, scientists and team members, each separately during their interviews, were invited to talk about the organization structure, administrative developments (such as job descriptions, organization charts, and the like), management meetings, and management style.

The organizations were mostly described as flat and informal, with all employees initially reporting to the CEO and two or more layers of management being added as the organization grew. Only in one case was such layering delayed until as many as 20 employees reported to the scientist-CEO. In the section on venture team formation, I indicated that 12 of the participants had attracted business partners into the company at its inception. In the majority of these cases this meant that, at some time after the inception of the company, the operational responsibility had been transferred to a nonscientist--in fact, an experienced CEO, COO or general manager. There were four cases where the venture's research and development function reported to both the CEO and the scientist, and this matrix arrangement was seen as a helpful, if sometimes time-consuming, aspect of organizational performance. Table 5-10, "Management Meetings and Management Style," was derived from the inputs received from scientists and team members; it shows that the workings of these young organizations were relatively free of routine conflicts, although most ventures have adopted prescribed patterns for conflict resolution.

These vignettes provide some practical insights into the workings of organization and management processes in these firms. The objective of this part of the study was also to detect variables in these processes that might relate to the specific scientist-started nature of the ventures. The majority of the study participants report open, participatory management styles with the chief executive occasionally making final decisions when the management team has been unable to act on a specific issue. There was no apparent relationship, in this respect, between this process and the scientist acting as chief executive or in another capacity. Five of the participants did report a strong propensity for the management team to make decisions based on consensus only. Without this consensus, decisions would be delayed. One of the scientist-chief executives reported, "Forced decisions are not scientific!"

Table 5-10 Management Meetings and Management Style

Scientist' position 1= at inception 2= subsequently	Management Meetings	Management Styles
A 1)Co-Chairman 2)CEO	not regular, mostly monthly or more often as required	CEO driven,mostly shared team decisions; flat informal organiaztion; conflict resolution rarely through board
B CEO	frequently, often weekly; scheduled ad hoc	CEO tries consensus management but dominates; conflict resolution without delay by CEO
C 1) CEO 2) VP R&D	unstructured, unscheduled, often weekly; monthly employee meetings	informal,participatory,consensus oriented; conflict resolution through discussion, rarely through CEO decision
D CEO	none; ad hoc meetings with staff, as required	task oriented vs. time oriented, participative and delegatory
E VP Science	weekly meetings per schedule	informal, team oriented but decisively led by CEO; ultimate conflict resolution by CEO
F 1)President 2)Chairman	monthly; board meeting also serves as management meeting	board by consensus; open management style; final decisions by President
G President/CEO	twice per month with preset agenda	open, autonomy for managers; conflicts resolved by management meeting
H President	no management team	all decisions by president
I President/CEO	VPs or president calls; held once a week to once a month	informal, open, participatory style; power shared with mgt. team; CEO resolves conflicts

J	1) VP Science 2) President	ad hoc only; frequent; often too long	mostly participative,sometimes dictatorial; often conflicts between venture partners
K	Scientist/ Director	weekly: including staff, officers and scientist	completely by consensus, decisions will be postponed until full agreement reached
L	Scientist- Director	every third week, or more frequently	informal, consensus oriented, participative: if no agreement, delay and discuss again
M	1)President 2)CEO/CSO	not initially, then once a month	participatory, interactive,open; unilateral decisions by president rarely required
N	CEO/Director	informal only	directive; people manage them- selves well; if required CEO resolves conflicts
O	Chairman	daily by phone with President; weekly with management team	informal, open, listen, then make decisions; final resolu- tion by President or Chairman
P	1)Pres/Scientist 2)Scientist- Director	weekly	originally participatory,team oriented; new president directive, top down approach
Q	President	originally not scheduled, then weekly meetings	autonomy oriented, lacking decisiveness, consistency; conflicts not always resolved
R	President	weekly, scheduled since general manager joined	directive, allowing rational arguments; President makes all final decisions
S	Pres/CEO	none; no management group defined	President resolves all issues and acts as facilitator
T	President	not initially, then every week	informal, interactive,allowing autonomy;still directive in task setting

U	VP R&D	informal meetings only	particpatory; conflicts (not frequent) resolved through discussion
V	1)CEO/Scientist 2)Scientist	weekly; sheduled, long meetings	participatory, aiming for consensus but also very directive at times; high standards

Team members seemed to accept this management concept as a valid and appealing input by the scientists. However, they also thought that for some decisions, or in the longer term, this procedure would not be in the interest of the business. For example, in one case, a business team member felt that the consensus approach was responsible for continuing the perfection of the technology in excess of market quality demands, thus prolonging a process which used up too many resources. In a few cases, directive or dictatorial management styles were observed but no relationship between these and the scientist origin of the venture could be found.

Eleven participating ventures also discussed organizational crisis situations. These invariably related to conflicts within the top management team or the board of directors. The results of such conflicts usually included the departure of either the scientist \or a business partner or professional manager from the CEO or COO position. In the former case, the originating scientist always remained involved with the business in some role, such as Chief Scientific Officer or Director. In the latter case, usually the departing executive or partner would make a clean break with the company. Table 5-11 further outlines the perceptions of the interviewed scientists and team members in these cases of organizational and management conflict.

The enumeration of conflicts, as seen by the scientists and team members, indicates a common trend in the source of these struggles. When a common venture mission, vision, or objective among the leading team is no longer present, conflicts arise and seemingly can only be resolved with the departure of one of the players or a change in position. These situations usually pitted a scientist against a businessman. As one partner put it: "Comparing the MBA and the scientist cultures shows some real extremes. Neither of these extremes is prepared to really listen, face the other's point of view when they have started a company together. They focus really well on functionally oriented tasks but really never cross the cultural gap between them."

Table 5-11. Venture Management Conflicts

Scientist's Perspective	Team Member's Perspective
A Scientist resigned as chief executive finding Board risk aversive.	Insufficient integration of the business and science objectives of the company.
B Board wanted scientist-executive turn operational responsibility over to a COO.	Not easy to accept for scientist who believes to have self-taught all business skills needed.
C Scientist restarted venture giving CEO position to new partner/ experienced executive.	Introduce more purpose oriented organization; take scientist out of operational line.
E Scientist and partner decided early to bring in professional business executive.	When executive introduced, conflicts between partner and executive arose, partner left.
J Business partner/CEO had to leave venture after scientist-partner relationship deteriorated.	Scientists had no business experience; caused many struggles, lack of common vision.
M President did not work out as he "excluded" the scientist-founder from the management process.	Conflict basis was scientist not understanding professional management standards and objectives.
N Scientist attracted business manager but let him go soon due to lack of technological understanding.	Learned that it is better to develop business skills within the company! Common goals!
P Executive joined as President but his objectives soon deviated from the scientist's. Was fired!	Learned too late how completely divergent scientists' and businessman's goals were.
Q Executive hired to organize systems and marketing efforts; was effective but left soon.	Team spirit, balanced skills and goals missing among scientist/owners; counterproductive!
S Attracted business partner; left venture soon. Scientist not a 'team person'!	

| V | When new partners came in, scientist lost interest, perceived lack of R&D commitment, left the venture. | Scientist could have stayed, misjudged the motives of the new team. |

It is my observation that the lack of synchronization of entrepreneurial objectives is the predominant cause of such problems. What, in turn, is the cause of the absence of common objectives? On the surface there might appear to be many plausible and functionally or behaviorally defined causes not specifically related to the scientist-started nature of the organization. Behind these explanations, however, I observed in each of these organizations a lack of attention--from the exploration and planning through to the management stages-- to the need to understand and bridge the cultural differences between scientists and business people. These inherent cultural differences place further emphasis on the need to define the organization's mission and objectives from the beginning, and to assure commitment from all members to these goals. Bartunek and Betters-Reed,[7] as discussed in chapter 2, emphasize the relationship between planning and organizational performance, and I restate their enumeration of critical issues:

• Creativity and thoroughness of the planning process
• Depth of commitment of the originator and planners to the organization
• Internal dynamics among originator and planners
• Quality of planner's relationship with the environment

The thoroughness with which these tasks are carried out will affect the success of the organization. In the conflict situations illustrated here, two areas in particular were not properly addressed. A shared commitment to the organization, its mission and goals was absent. Also lacking was a healthy dynamic between the scientist and members of the team.

The organization and management processes in the scientist-started firms require careful planning and attention, just as in any other type of business. However, due to the very diverse backgrounds from which teams are formed in a scientist-started venture, the likelihood of conflicts would be much increased if goal setting, planning, team member selection, and team management were not adequately prepared and guided. That process requires, above all, what was reviewed previously and described by Adizes as Integration skills.

5.10   Driving and Restraining Forces Shaping Venture Success

Throughout this chapter, the field studies have been analyzed for the processes of venture planning, inception, and management, with a view to explore which variables might be critical in determining organizational performance. Furthermore, a central question has been, "Which variables might be unique to the scientist-started nature of the new firm?" Before the conclusion of this chapter, the relationship between these various factors and the performance of the venture will be examined. To lay the foundation for improved understanding in this area, we again start with a review of how the players in these ventures themselves perceived the major driving and restraining forces shaping organi -zational success. Table 5-12 illustrates the most commonly felt driving and restraining influences and, in additional, contrasts ones felt by the scientists with those of the team members.

A pattern of common understanding between the scientist and the venture member regarding the firms' driving and restraining forces could not be established. Of the driving forces, only 16% concerned issues that were mentioned in the same firm by both the scientist and the venture member. Half of those expressed agreement on the validity of the science involved. In the area of restraining forces, commonly mentioned issues amounted to only 9%. Half of those agreed that lack of funding was a restraining force. Thus, although scientist and non-scientist partners agreed on science as a driving force and on lack of financing as a restraining force, this unanimity concerned only a small proportion of the issues mentioned in the participating ventures.

The assumption could be made that in a venture with a consensus-based team management structure, a high level of agreement about critical issues could affect the success of the firm. In such a situation, both interviewees could be expected to indicate a related pattern of driving and restraining forces. However, I have to conclude that insufficient evidence exists to support this line of thinking. Few of the companies were subject to consensus management. Second, division of the various functional tasks would, even in the case of consensus management, tend to influence the selection and priority of issues mentioned. Therefore we cannot draw any conclusions on the basis of inter-venture comparisons.

Table 5-12. Perceived Driving and Restraining Forces Shaping Venture Success

	Scientists(n=22)	Team members (n=19)
Driving Forces		
Validity of the science/scientist reputation	16	10
Availability of funding	7	10
Availability of business/management skills	8	7
Qualified venture team, team spirit	7	8
Attractive market opportunities	8	10
Support from third parties	8	4
Financial rewards	1	2
Facilities	1	-
Patents	1	1
Various other	6	4
Total	63	56
RetrainingForces		
Problems with the science	5	4
Lack of funding	9	14
Insufficient business/management skills	9	8
Poor venture team, poor team spirit	6	6
Poor market opportunities	4	1
Lack of third party support	4	5
"Money culture"	6	-
Lack of time, time lost	4	3
Lawsuit	2	2
Facilities	2	-
Regulatory requirements	2	-
Other	5	-
Total	58	43

With respect to the frequency with which scientists and venture members mentioned the various driving and restraining forces, a more conclusive picture emerges. Science and the scientist's reputation as connected to the venture were the driving forces most frequently mentioned (by almost three-quarters of the scientists). The next most frequently identified driving forces mentioned by the scientists concerned business skills and market opportunities (36%). In contrast, the team members reported a more evenly distributed appreciation of issues critical to success. Half of them mentioned science, funding, and market opportunities as driving forces towards venture success. Venture team quality was mentioned by over 40%. Team members thus display a functionally more balanced picture than scientists concerning the positive forces that will contribute to the success of the venture. Scientists are more frequently concerned with the scientific and technological aspects of venture success. This finding is in line with the observed absence of business skills among scientists, as well as their tendency, noted in this field study as well as the literature, toward technology domination.

In regard to restraining forces, the conclusions are not as clear-cut. Scientists and venture team members most frequently mention both the lack of funding and the lack of business skills. Forty percent of the scientists mention lack of funding while almost 80% of team members note this restraining force. Among the potentially critical factors holding back the enterprise from its objectives, venture team members, mostly businessmen who can be expected to be closer to the business and financial issues than scientists, will note lack of financial resources more often than do the scientists.

"Money culture" relates to comments made by scientists with respect to what they see as the distracting influence on organizational performance of partners, managers, and financiers who express money as a final goal to the exclusion of all other objectives. This is another example of the differing values among scientists and businessmen.

5.11   Evaluation of Venture Performance

To obtain an impression of the venture performance evaluation, the scientists and team members were asked to provide a rating for enterprise performance as well as an indication of the most significant thing they would have, in hindsight, done differently. This approach not only provided insights into how the organizational performance was evaluated by the venture partners themselves; it also allowed them to see what, if anything, the venture players learned from their experiences. The evaluation overview in Table 5-13 is supplemented by a few statements from the investigator describing the year of commencement, the type of management, and the current financial situation of the firm.

Table 5-13. Venture Evaluation

Performance Evaluation	The single item done differently if venture could start over again	Researcher's Comments
scale 1 thru 7 1=compl below 4=as expected 7=compl above	s=scientist response (n=22) t=team member response (n=19)	year of start/ year restart; profitability; current CEO; scientist or entrepreneur/businessman
A s=2 t=4	s=select better board, less intellectual more risk/purpose oriented t=firm less science dominated	1978; not profitable; previous CEO scientist-founder; businessman/ CEO since 1984
B s=5 t=7	s=control marketing/sales personnel, do not understand them! t=control marketing/sales	1978; profit forecasted for 1989; scientist-founder-CEO
C s=6 t=4	s= more market research & funding, employee management training! t= engineering team, scientist not in operations	1978/1987; profitable;initial CEO was scientist-founder; businessman/CEO since 1987
D s=7	s=possibly earlier funding, tradeoff would be loss of independence	1985; product launched 1989; scientist-founder-CEO
E s=6 t=6	s= professional management from venture inception t=prof. management from start	1981; profitable; businessman/CEO since 1983
F s=7 t=5	s=more personal money in firm, stronger in dealings w. university t=cash flow producing activities	1988; R&D contracting; profitability not known; scientist-CEO (founder's assoc)
G s=1 t=1	s=marketing skills from the start t=more capital to start	1982; firm folded 1989 lack of funds; scientist-founder-CEO
H s=7	s=no change!	1988; R&D stage company; scientist-CEO
I s=7 t=4	s=less board seats to university! t=no change at all	1986; not profitable yet; scientist-founder-CEO

J	s=3 t=3	s=start with management team: scientists to focus on science! t= venture in suitable location	1983; not profitable; scientist-founder-CEO; previous CEO, business partner
K	s=6 t=4	s=more "business" preparation t=better administrative structure	1986; product marketed 1989; engineer-CEO (founder's assoc)
L	s=4 t=4	s=stronger management t=leadership skills; science/ operations communication!	1988; R&D contracting; not profitable; businessman-CEO
M	s=7 t=6	s=know money/funding from very start; critcal preparation t=no change	1970/1983; profitable; businessmen-CEO's since 1984
N	s=7 t=7	s=do exactly the same t=no changes	1978; profitable; scientist-founder-CEO
O	s=7 t=7	s=sell earlier vs. continuing perfection; t=exactly the same	1972/1978; profitable; firm sold 1984; businessman-CEO
P	s=7 t=7	s=would start only for funding opportunity. t=caution choosing CEO/selecting financial partners	1987 /89 firm made dormant pending funding/ mgt conflict; businessman-CEO
Q	s=7 t=1	s= no partners, stay with tech. expertise. t=scientist out earlier	1984; firm sold in crisis; scientist-founder-CEO
R	s=4 t=4	s= hire R&D mgr & people mgt skills. t=systematic funding	1985; lack of funding; scientist-founder CEO
S	s=4	s=marketing staff/develop market. plan from start of venture	1982; not profitable; scientist/ engineer/founder-CEO
T	s=4 t=2	s=prof. people management t=pursue distrib. aggressively	1982; profitable; scientist-founder-CEO
U	s=6 t=3	s=no change, t=delay start till funded ; no cut back in R&D	1987; R&D firm, no profit; businessman-CEO since 1988
V	s=2 t=3	s=no funding from venture capitalists. develop firm slowly t=more strategic options	1983; dvlpmt firm, no profits; Scientist-founder prior CEO; businessman-CEO since 1987

Scientists' mean performance rating was 5.3, or "better than expected", with 41% finding their venture's track record "completely above expectations." Team members appeared more conservative in this evaluation with a mean of 4.3, or just above "as expected", and only four members reported their experience as "completely above expectations." Over one-half of the interviewed partners and team members noted, in retrospect, that they would pay more attention to business and management skills at the start of a new venture. In this respect, such needs as a balanced business-science orientation, as well as funding, marketing, administrative, and people management skills were mentioned. In contrast, there was no mention of a need for more science and technology skills or investment in these areas at the outset of a new enterprise. The experiences which the participants had in planning and managing a scientist-started business had impressed these various needs on them to the extent that they mentioned these items as the single most urgent thing they would, in hindsight, do differently.

Six participants indicated that they would make no changes at all before restarting this kind of venture. Neither the indication of "no change" nor that of the desirability of more management skills appeared to correlate with the venture's performance record, as perceived by the participants or as compared to venture development or profitability. I would postulate that the strongest impetus for deciding that a key item had to be done differently from the outset would primarily relate to the participants' personal entrepreneurial experiences and, to a lesser extent, to expectations for venture success or profitability.

During the exploratory field studies, three of the participating enterprises changed dramatically in character, as a result of their organizational and business performance. Company G, although with many technological irons in the entrepreneurial fire, simply ran out of funding due to a lack of ability to turn know-how into cash flow. Both participants'\low ratings of the venture's performance were congruent with this shutdown. Venture P put itself in a dormant situation, laying off all employees and deferring all expenses until a management and funding crisis could be resolved. A major conflict had arisen with the businessman-CEO over long term objectives as well as the fund-raising performance of this research stage company, leading to the separation of the executive. In this firm, the study participants still rated the performance as substantially above expectations in view of what had been accomplished prior to the crisis. The third venture that underwent major changes, company Q, was taken over by a much larger company when this startup firm overexpanded in uncharted technological areas and markets and financially overextended itself. In this case, the scientist still rated the firm's performance as very high, although professional achievement and business success were not demonstrated.

Only in one other company (S) did I consider the participants' rating of their venture performance incongruent with organizational progress and profitability. Here, a small, fully self financing company had grown steadily and been profitable since 1983, but the partners rated it low in view of their much higher expectations.

5.12   Scientific and Business Cultures

Throughout the conducting of the field studies, incidental comments were made by scientists and team members regarding the differences in the professional cultures between scientists and business people. These differences were perceived to influence the venture processes significantly, and I have arranged them here into four main categories:

• **Planning**.   Scientists noted the generally longer planning horizons they work with in technological development as compared with those of their business colleagues. To them, the entrepreneurs and business partners appeared preoccupied with short-term performance pressures and often tried to force these pressures upon the science and technology departments of their ventures. Technological development was sometimes seen by the business members as excessively long lasting, leading to a perfectionism beyond market demands.

• **Risk**.   Although, as reported, a significant number of the scientists put their own money at risk in the initial venture funding stage, they were nevertheless found by other team members to be risk averse in terms of making decisions. Was it the investment of their personal funds that contributed to this risk aversion? The answer to this question could not be ascertained. Scientists thought that risks could be minimized by rational "scientific" approaches to those problems demanding decisions, while business partners felt that they had to move ahead and make a decision, usually on the basis of imperfect information.

• **Management styles**.   Consensus management and an egalitarian approach to decisions was a tendency reported by some ventures. "If consensus cannot be reached, the venture team is not ready for a decision and postponement then lasts until everybody is ready." Or, "A forced decision cannot be a scientific decision." Businessmen saw themselves as far more purpose-oriented and focused than scientists. "Somebody has to make the decision here, so we can get on with it."

• **Money.** This area had the most severe comments, made by the scientists who frequently could not understand the mentality of money-motivated people. Venture capitalists, in their quest for capital gains and income, were felt to be uninterested in the intrinsic value of the technology. Greed was sometimes suspected. The system of sales commissions was also felt to motivate the sales and marketing groups in a very one-sided way. Some ventures reported difficulties in convincing outside scientists to cooperate with their firm and accept that working with a company team does not lower them to the money making motive. Scientists expecially disliked outside pressures from financial stakeholders for short-term results.

These differing values were not the only potential sources of friction in the ventures; the comparative expectations of these groups also further increased the risk of conflicts. The anthropologist Dubinskas illustrates this point in his study on science and management cultures: "In their native habitats, both scientists and managers are high-status individuals used to running their own show."[8] In the firms in this study, as was noted in the discussion of conflicts in the ventures, scientists and business partners are often pitted against each other.

5.13   Summary

This chapter started with the question of how scientists initially arrived at a commercial vision for their scientific work. It appeared that, although three-quarters of the participants reported defining the first commercial vision themselves, this process was always facilitated through some kind of interaction with the "outside," nonscience world. Of course, another important contributing factor in leading the scientist to imagine commercial applications was the degree of his personal inclination toward exploring practical applications or even commercial ideas. In chapter 4, the often cited correlation between the entrepreneurial endeavors of the father and the likelihood that the son-- particularly the first born son--would engage in similar activities, was confirmed in this research.

This leads to the scientist's motivation in going further than simply defining a commercial vision to that of deciding to play a role in that implementation process. Over 85% of the participants mentioned the advancement of science and its application as their prime motivation, and over 80% mentioned the opportunity to play a personal role in building a business. The third most frequently mentioned perspective in desiring an entrepreneurial or business role dealt with the opportunity to make money and build equity. The motivations of the scientists in joining or starting a venture appeared to match closely the roles that they subsequently played. The drive to build a successful business, make money and enhance the science and its application coincided with the Entrepreneuring and Produce roles they played.

The backgrounds that the participating scientists offered, in terms of business experience and business training, appeared minimal. As expected, on the basis of the definition of scientist which was used, only two participants were found to have had prior business experience. None of the scientists had been enrolled in business training courses, although more than one-half of them recognized this as a critical need at some point in the life of the venture. The most frequently reported skills lacking were in the area of team and people management. The inherent contradiction in these findings is that nothing was done to address the scientist's need for business training. To explain this contradiction between need and action, factors should be conidered such as (1) the scientist's inclination to learn by self-study, (2) the tendency for science and technology to dominate in the venture, and 3) the low priority given training among all venture tasks.

If the technology-related tasks are grouped, they comprise two-thirds of all tasks mentioned. The only business task that could compete with technology, in terms of the emphasis given to it by the scientists, was funding. Although business and strategic planning are critical in successful funding, scientists attached low importance to these tasks. Funding or money issues were also often mentioned as the area over which the different behavioral and cultural backgrounds of scientists and businessmen would clash. Funding and the need for a return on investment exemplified the often-cited shorter term and goal-oriented focus of the businessman and the entrepreneur. This is in contrast with the wider purpose of the quest for knowledge and the longer time frame in which scientists tend to express their visions. Entrepreneurship and management were thus not recognized by the scientist as serious disciplines; science and technology dominate. An example here is that technology assessment was either formally or informally carried out in the early venture stages by over 70% of the participants, often in conjunction with government grant applications. Market assessments were completed in less than one-quarter of the ventures, often as part of an outside funding drive.

In the process of team formation, this emphasis on technical issues shows in the use of primarily functional criteria in hiring or attracting team members. Personality and fit within the group were not often considered in building the venture team. The majority of the businesses in the study did not bring professional management on board until a later stage in the venture. Science and technology were consistently well represented in these ventures. In terms of Adizes' model, however, the ventures appeared short in Produce skills, through lack of marketing and distribution skills, and in Integration skills, through lack of people and team management skills.

Scientists were found to be entrepreneurs in the true sense of the word in putting their own funds at risk in the venture. In fact, three-quarters of the scientists reported investing in the initial stage of their venture. Tension was observed between the scientist's desire to retain independence, on the one hand, and the availability of adequate funds to develop the vision, on the other. The timing of the venture start was, in the majority of the cases, determined by funding availability.

In the area of venture organization, no inconsistent trends were discerned that would distinguish scientist-started firms from other new ventures, with the exception of the previously mentioned science and technology domination of the organization. Consensus management and a sense that forced or autocratic decisions are not a scientific way to make decisions, were reported in the earlier stages of five of the ventures, and this notion appears specifically related to the scientist-started nature of these firms. Eleven ventures did report serious organizational conflicts, resulting in partners leaving or their positions in the firm being redefined. These conflicts arose in all cases as a result of a lack of intensive and detailed planning for common goals and objectives among the team members of the venture. The very diverse individual backgrounds from which teams were usually formed in scientist-started firms further increased the chances of conflict in the absence of a common base of venture values and objectives. These differences in the professional cultures between business people and scientists played a significant role in venture team management processes.

In the assessment of driving and restraining forces shaping success, as well as in the venture performance evaluation, both scientists and team members underscored, in retrospect, the need for more business and management skills at the start of the new venture. Team members displayed a functionally more balanced picture than scientists concerning the positive forces that will contribute to the success of the venture. Scientists were more frequently concerned with the scientific and technological aspects of venture success.

5.14   Conclusions

1. Scientists are attracted to playing entrepreneurial and managerial roles in science-based ventures, in view of their needs to advance and apply their science, build businesses, and obtain monetary rewards. Scientists will put their own money and resources at risk to start their ventures.

2. In evaluating which skills scientists personally could use in their entre preneurial endeavors, most scientists sooner or later during the development of the firm, identify their personal need for business training, mostly in areas of team and people management, as well as for financing. As the firm evolves, this need is reported more frequently and keeps the scientists from achieving the organizational results they strive for. Yet they appear unable to implement these business and management training plans.

3. Irrespective of their own training desires and needs, scientists and their team members frequently conclude that professional management skills are missing from their venture teams. In this respect they particularly identify the need for productive business and team integrative skills.

4. Although the symptoms of differences in professional cultures that make up the venture team are frequently recognized, few ventures consciously address the need for establishing a common venture culture which could bridge different values and objectives. Often, new members to the team are attract- ed on the basis of functional skills only, neglecting personal chemistry within the team. Management conflicts are frequently rooted in a lack of common objectives, mission, and planning horizons among the team members.

5. Scientist-started ventures are frequently found to be heavily science-and technology-dominated in organization, management processes, and resource allocation. The main emphasis in these firms is on technology generation and other productive and entrepreneurial activities. This is not to imply that this approach is wrong; in fact, such focus is a critical requirement in science based venture development, but technology domination, at the

expense of other business activities impairs the venture's ability to develop in a stable and profitable fashion.

The scientist-entrepreneur displays a duality in his assessment of entrepreneurship. On the one hand, he readily and personally accepts the challenge and the risks that these activities imply. On the other hand, he resists some of the learning and tasks required and often rejects the values and attitudes with which business will confront him. How do successful scientist-entrepreneurs reconcile these apparent contradictions and organize around these obstacles? For the purpose of this study, organizational performance was previously defined as the manner and degree in which entrepreneurial and management processes contribute to the achievement of organizational objectives of the enterprise.

Five scientist-entrepreneurs and their ventures could be identified who had demonstrated better organizational performance than the remaining participants. In addition to substantially reaching the objectives they set for themselves, these participating scientists and team members valued their ventures as successful and these firms were profitable. With respect to profitability, this was derived from published financials or from information supplied by the ventures themselves. In the latter case, confirmation of profitability was obtained from third parties. In addition to dedicated scientists who contributed valued science and technology to the new firm, what did these scientist-started ventures have in common? These successful ventures displayed a number of common characteristics and concerns which had been consistently attended to during the early development stages. In the following, the number shown in parenthesis is the number of ventures with these characteristics and concerns.

• Recognition by the scientist of personal strengths and weaknesses in relation to venture management (5).
• Scientist put his own resources at risk towards starting the venture (5).
• Scientist made an effort to expose himself to critical business issues such as funding and market strategies; attracted missing skills through partners or team members (5).
• Scientist facilitated team formation and integration, assured commitment to common goals and mutual respect among team members, or insured that a partner attended to the task of team management (4).
• Cultural differences within scientist-started ventures and the need for common values and mission were recognized in the venture team (3).

In part III of this book, I will propose a model for the scientist-started venture on the basis of the theoretical and empirical research presented in this and previous chapters.

Reference notes

1. Drucker, Peter F. *Innovation and Entrepreneurship Practice and Principles.* New York: Harper & Row Publishers, 1985.
2. Dubinskas, Frank A. "Janus Organizations: Scientists and Managers In Genetic Engineering Firms." In: *Making Time, Ethnographies of High-Technology Organizations*, Edited by Dubinskas, Frank A. Philadelphia: Temple University Press, 1988, p.197.
3. Adizes, Ichak. "Organizational Passages: Diagnosing and Treating Lifecycle Problems of Organizations." *Organizational Dynamics*, Summer 1979.
4. Timmons, Jeffry A. with Smollen, Leonard E. and Dingee, Alexander L.M., Jr. *New Venture Creation, A Guide To Entrepreneurship.* Homewood, Illinois: Irwin, 1985. p.14.
5. Adizes, op cit.
6. Roberts, Edward B. "What We've Learned: Managing Invention and Innovation." *Research-Technology Management*, Vol 31, January/February 1988, p. 13.
7. Bartunek, Jean M. and Betters-Reed, Bonita L. "The Stages of Organizational Creation." *American Journal of Community Psychology*, Vol 15, No.3, 1987.
8. Dubinskas, Frank A. "The Culture Chasm: Scientists and Managers in Genetic-Engineering Firms." *Technology Review*, Vol 88, May/June 1985. p. 27.

Chapter 6

UNIVERSITY RELATIONSHIPS AND COMPARATIVE ASPECTS OF SCIENTISTS AS ENTREPRENEURS

6.1 Introduction

The previous chapter presented an in-depth review of the planning and management experiences of the participants in this research. In carrying out this study, a number of additional issues were encountered which, although not directly fitting our main theme, should nevertheless be mentioned since they contribute to a general understanding of the phenomenon of the scientist-entrepreneur and his firm. Observations were made through the field studies and covered the issues of technology transfer, the scientists' relationships with the universities, and U.S.-Canadian comparative aspects of scientist-started ventures. The purpose of this chapter is to report these findings and place them in the context of prior research and existing literature. The following sections will elaborate on these issues.

6.2 Technology Transfer
6.3 The Decision to Leave the University
6.4 U.S.-Canadian Comparative Aspects
6.5 Summary

6.2   Technology Transfer and University-Industry Relations

What are some of the key motivations of the scientist-entrepreneur in respect to his relationship with the university? From the interviews I compiled, the following typical professorial "wish list" emerged. From the point of view of the scientists, these items, not listed in any particular order, would be beneficial to both parties, providing equity, licensing income, and long-term faculty commitment to the university.

• Venture funding or other forms of resource involvement by the university;
• Continued meaningful relationship with the university;
• Where necessary, transfer of university technology rights to the venture.

Technology transfer defines the policies and practices by which scientific and technological information can be transferred from the university or research organization to existing or new industrial entities. In a wider sense, this subject can be defined in terms of university-industry relationships. In the United States and particularly in Canada, a great deal of effort has been spent in recent years in an attempt to substantially improve the relationships between universities, industry, and government. Link and Tassey have characterized progress in the United States as follows: "The significant apathy that characterized relationships between industry and universities and the adversarial nature of relationships between industries and government have both faded rapidly in the 1980s as the realities of global competition have surfaced in the United States."[1] The realities of competition have long motivated both provincial and federal governments in Canada to support the building of these relationships, particularly with an eye to high technology development. Whether the diminution of apathy noted by Link and Tassey has already started to translate into tangible results is an open question. It should be noted that, in terms of government support for technology-based innovation and entrepreneurship, both the United States and Canada have had attractive grant programs in place during the 1980s. In view of the current high levels of interest among universities in technology development and transfer, this area represents a field of academic study with much potential. However, it falls outside the scope of this book to elaborate in general theoretical and practical terms on university-industry relationships.

Therefore, the objective of this section is to provide a basic level of background information regarding technology transfer and to review aspects of university-industry relationships specifically from the perspective of entrepreneurial faculty and their dealings with universities and research institutions.

The form that such relationships and transfers can take will vary considerably. They extend from outright technology transfer through license agreements, to cooperative research agreements between universities and companies, and to direct financial university involvement through the use of university venture funds. Geisler and Rubenstein,[2] in their recent review of university-industry relations, report that although there have been many reports, conferences, and descriptions of particular relationships, relatively little *research* literature has come out on this subject. It is interesting to note that university-industry relationships have often been defined in terms of the *problems* of such relationships as opposed to their *opportunities*. Geisler and Rubenstein[3] summarized the major issues they observed:

Major Issues in University-Industry Relations

1. Inherent differences in mission and objectives;
2. Differences in organizational structure and policies;
3. Differences in orientation and interests of individual researchers;
4. Effectiveness of university-industry arrangements and mechanisms for collaboration;
5. Benefits versus costs;
6. How to evaluate university-industry interaction.

This enumeration is useful in that it also leads to all the questions which the universities and enterprising faculties of this study sooner or later had to confront.

One albeit narrowly defined indication that university-industry relations have not yet widely flourished in a monetary sense is shown by the paucity of institutions that have derived significant royalty income from their technological innovations. Table 6-1, based on an analysis by Buderi[4], illustrates this point. It is noteworthy that in only ten universities in the United States has technology transfer produced revenues in excess of $1 million per year.

The *problem* orientation was reflected in the relationships reported by the scientists who participated in this study. In the case of the scientist-entrepreneur, the scientist typically discusses a proposal with his institution to transfer technology to an entity which he represents or in which he will play a role. In this context, the scientist might plan to stay on in his university position, propose a reduced form of involvement with the university, or leave entirely after the transfer has been completed. The first two approaches have, in

themselves, generated some discussion of the potential advantages and disadvantages faced by entrepreneurial faculty members.

Table 6-1. Top Revenue Producing Universities

University	$ (millions)	Big Hit(s) 1987	Patents filed
Stanford University	9.2	Cohen/Boyer	42
University of Wisconsin	8+	Vitamin D	*
MIT	5.5	Magnetic Core Memory Synthetic Penicillin	66
University of California	5.4	•	65
University of Florida	3.9	Gatorade	13
Michigan State University	3.3	Cisplatin	*
Columbia University	2.5	•	*
University of Houston	1.6	superconductivity	*
Harvard University	1.2	•	*
Cornell University	1.2	Paravirus Vaccine	29

• No dominant patent.
* Less than 13 patents filed in 1987.
From The Scientist, December 12, 1988.

Richter[5] reviewed a number of *potential sources of conflict* that may
arise when scientists have dual loyalties such as the choice to direct research
activities to the university laboratories or to the research facility operated by the
scientist's venture. Indeed, conflicts of interest and issues of ethics do
occasionally arise and, in some extreme cases, come into the spotlight of public
news.[6] Although other potential conflicts exist, advantages also appear when the
institution demonstrates flexibility on such issues as funding or retaining
faculty. This section can only summarize some of the key questions which are
being asked in regard to the changing relationships between universities and
industrial organizations, including scientist-started new ventures. A first
approach to a complete review of these matters was published by Etzkowitz[7] in
1983 and provides a clear description of the issues at play. Against this
potentially controversial background, many universities have been slow to adopt
clear policies regarding technology transfer. Geisler and Rubenstein enumerate
the many cultural, structural and philosophical differences that do exist between
universities and business enterprises.

When the lack of clear policies to deal with entrepreneurial scientists is added to this picture, the often cited less-than-successful relationships between scientists and their universities come into focus.

A prime motivation for universities to consider when entering into technology transfer is the expectation of a source of funding. There are a multitude of structures that transfer arrangements can use. I have defined three main groups describing most transfer agreements.

1. The licensing agreement. Typically, the licensee's staff might work on further development of the technology, with university scientists sometimes brought in as required on a consulting basis. In return for the use of university technology as disclosed, a royalty is received.

2. University-industry cooperative research agreements. University research staff and those of the industrial partner work together on development. Financial return to the university might come in the form of royalties, payment for research work, or in other arrangements.

3. University venture funds. In recent years, some universities have, through venture funds in which they have a stake or which they control, invested university funds in ventures that aim to exploit technology developed in their laboratories. Scientists and third parties are usually also stakeholders in such ventures. Equity appreciation of the ventures and royalties are the forms through which university venture funds expect to be remunerated.

The scientist-entrepreneur and his venture might function within any of these approaches. The third model, university venture funds, financially and philosophically requires the most profound commitments from the university. Dinces,[8] in a 1989 presentation on university venture funds, reported that in recent years Washington University, the University of Chicago, Johns Hopkins University, Boston University, and Harvard University have become involved with university venture funds. The degree of direct involvement is usually expressed in the degree of arm's length with which the fund operates in relation to the funding university. The questions of university philosophy, and the potential conflicts of interests of scientists, as discussed earlier in this section, remain the same. Dinces postulates that what sets university venture funds apart from other approaches to commercialization is that they may allow for the development of technologies that might not otherwise happen due to the short-term demands for return on capital inherent in most other sources of seed funding.

In the process of their establishment, university venture funds force the development of clear policies and procedures relating to university involvement in ventures and the position of their faculty within such structures. However, the majority of universities have not gone this far in defining and operating technology transfer. The absence of a purposeful strategy to pursue these matters frequently results from unresolved discussions about university value systems. Consider, for instance, such basic questions as the pursuit of knowledge versus the pursuit of funding, or concerns about the scientist's dual loyalties, and it can be understood that scientist-university dealings often appear transacted in a climate short of philosophical and procedural definition. In such situations the scientist may then have to deal with a technology transfer director, a patent attorney, or an administrator of the university who must operate in a relative policy vacuum. Technology transfer problems often arose under such circumstances for our sample of scientists. Table 6-2 illustrates the experiences reported in this research.

Table 6-2. Scientist's Experiences in University Relations

University positively supported venture creation	6	(37%)
Entrepreneurial activities not supported or discouraged	10	(63%)
n=16		

Six of the ventures in this research did not require the support of universities or research organizations because the technology was developed outside the institution or did not require any university transfer approvals. Of those ventures where the scientist did enlist university cooperation in technology transfer, two-thirds reported negative experiences. The most often voiced comments related to the perceived lack of interest by the university in considering the opportunity and a reluctance to formally or informally support the proposed activities. The absence of a stated position on where the institution stood in regard to technology transfer, or on university scientists taking on entrepreneurial roles was perceived to be the basis for this attitude. Most scientists reported as unproductive their dealings with administrative university staff, who were perceived as short-sighted and lacking vision.

All the participants who reported positive relations with their universities in the venture creation phase dealt with institutions where university policies for technology transfer and outside activities of faculty had been clearly defined and communicated. In half of these positively ranked cases, the university or research institution had, in fact, through its venture fund, taken a financial position in the new venture.

6.3   The Decision to Leave the University

The decision to leave the university, or to modify that relationship in the course of the venture's development was an important personal issue for many of the scientists in this study.   This section reviews the various aspects of that decision.

Although each individual scientist's experiences are unique, I concluded from the research interviews that a key issue commonly shared by almost all scientist-entrepreneurs related to their employment status at the time of the venture start. These scientists enjoyed secure employment situations within their institutions. Except in four instances where the scientist held part time or adjunct faculty positions, these scientists used the employment base at the university to explore their options.   Richter[9] and Martin[10] candidly refer to this phase as "professorial moonlighting" and "moonlighting," respectively.   This period was important in that it allowed the scientist time to carefully evaluate his technology commercialization structures and venture creation plans, as well as the nature of his longer term affiliation with the academic institution.

At the time of venture establishment, half of the scientists decided to join the new enterprise on a full-time basis.   Joining the venture full time usually meant reducing or eliminating involvement with the university.   At the time of this study, 14 scientists (64%) were in full-time employment with their enterprises, including one scientist who had also continued on a full-time basis with his university.   Eight scientists (36%) had served their firms on a part-time basis while maintaining full-time positions at their academic or research institutions.   In half the cases studied, scientists went through one or more periods during which they struggled with the limited ways available to them to shape and pursue their continuing career with the university.   Obviously, this personal issue was important.   In table 6-3, the scientists themselves comment on their relationships with the university or research institution.

Table 6-3. The Scientist's Relationship with the University

Scientist's Commentary

A. Scientist-founder instrumental in bringing various scientists to the venture. After two years gave up professorship to run venture himself. After three years, returned to university.

B. Scientist with government research institution gave up his position without much delay when opportunity arose to commercialize his technology.

C. University professor was torn for a number of years in choosing between venture and university. This delay reportedly affected venture performance. Eventually chose to leave university.

D. University professor, when occasion was right to leave and commercialize his science, took the step and did not look back. Would have preferred to maintain at least part-time relationship with university, but this option was not available.

E. Once the scientist had noted the market potential, he left the university as soon as the venture started.

F. Clinician and researcher wanted to get into applied science, technology transfer and entrepreneurship, and left institution as soon as the venture was established.

G. Scientist did not consider leaving his university professorship. Placed associates in the venture and played a role in it on a part- time basis.

H. Scientist planned all along to move out of research and run a science venture.

I. When scientist saw the opportunity to commercialize (his) science, he headed up the venture and left the university research institute immediately.

J. Scientists decided against return to academia, left research institution to start their own venture.

K. Scientist never intended to leave the university. Placed associates in the venture to run and manage it and spends time with venture on a part-time basis.

L. Scientists never considered leaving university. They play key role in the research and development management process; the company is run by business partners.

M. Scientist left research institute when conflict with other scientist arose. Torn whether to leave university and go full-time with venture or not. Eventually joined the venture full time.

N. Maintained full-time professorship at university while working practically full time at venture for many years. Recently gave up full-time university position.

O. The issue of giving up clinical work and university affiliation never arose. His partners and associates ran the company, the scientist provided leadership and input on a part-time basis.

P. Leaving the university was never an issue! The scientist worked in both university and venture laboratories. The only issue is the lack of time!

Q. The scientist decided to leave the university when he could not achieve there what he wanted and thus decided to start a private venture. Doing both was desirable but not an available option

---

R. The scientist maintains a full-time professorship and a CEO position. University should be more flexible about scientist-entrepreneurs as maintaining university position is mutually desirable.

S. Applied scientist worked on the technology at the university and then decided it was such an opportunity that he soon went full time with the venture and abandoned academic career aspirations.

T. Once the opportunity was seen, this scientist eventually started a venture and left. Would have preferred a university relationship; option was priced out of his range!

U. The venture was what scientist wanted, has almost given up all his activities at the university.

V. It was not a difficult decision to separate from the university. Scientist thinks, however that it could be mutually beneficial if scientist-entrepreneurs keep connections with their universities.

Many scientists experienced difficulty in deciding to disengage from their full-time position at their universities, even though the ventures appeared to demand full-time attention. In the ideal circumstance, they would have preferred to remain connected with their respective universities while pursuing their entrepreneurial activities. These scientist-entrepreneurs saw this approach as potentially attractive for both the universities and themselves in terms of continued scientific collaboration. In the final analysis, there were no cases, other than those situations where the scientists retained full-time positions with their universities, where creative solutions were found to keep scientist-entrepreneurs actively linked to their institutions.

6.4 U.S.-Canadian Comparative Aspects

This exploratory research covered scientist-entrepreneurs and their ventures in two countries. Throughout the conducting and analysis of the project, I checked for the possibility of variables that might be attributed to social and economic differences between these countries. There were eight participating ventures in Canada and 14 in the United States.

In reviewing the socio-economic parameters such as age, family background, and country of origin of the scientists, as reported in chapter 4, no findings were out of line with the expected tendencies identified in prior research. Neither did the study reveal any contradictory results when comparing these statistics between the Canadian and U.S. scientist-entrepreneurs. I did not further analyze the various numbers shown in chapter 4 on a comparative basis in view of the relatively small sample size. Any further analysis of the variations between Canadian and U.S. statistics would require a new study with a larger sample specifically aimed at measuring socio-economic data of this nature.

With respect to the entrepreneurial planning and management processes and the resulting organizational performance, the research did point to only one possible difference which would be rooted in differences between the countries of origin of these ventures. The issue here is the availability and receipt of government grants to conduct biomedical research in science-based new ventures. Five firms had received government grants at venture inception. At the time of the study this number had risen to 12. Table 6-4 shows the distribution of government grants among Canadian and US-based firms.

It is considered significant that *all* of the Canadian cases had received some form of government grant at the time of the study, while the U.S. participants reported a corresponding grant award rate of 29%.

Table 6-4. Government Grants Received

	Ventures		
	Canadian	U.S.	Total
Ventures in the study	8	14	22
Government grants received	8	4	12
Grant award rate	100%	29%	55%

It appeared from our field interviews and from the information received at the time of the planning of this study from Industry, Science and Technology Canada, the federal ministry in Canada looking after these matters, that the federal government possessed current knowledge of and maintained active working relationships with high technology firms in its support of technological development in Canada. Federal grants in Canada typically come through the National Research Council which also operates its own laboratories. At the provincial level, both Quebec and Ontario also offer various forms of support, including research and training grants, to their technology-based companies and new ventures. In contrast, the U.S. ventures that did receive research grants all did so from the U.S. federal government, usually through SBIR (Small Business Innovative Research Grants). There were no reports in this study of any technology development or research grants awarded by state governments.

6.5   Summary and Conclusions

Technology transfer and the wider issue of the scientist's relationship with the university during planning and establishment of the new firm are mostly defined in terms of a *problem orientation*. Both the literature and the findings of this research point to a lack or a perceived lack of definition among universities and research institutions of philosophical and procedural approaches to commercializing technology. To be sure, the questions facing academic and research organizations are not easy; they relate to the very core mission of these institutions. Do commercial links, sooner or later, interfere with the pursuit of knowledge? Are faculty who get involved with setting up ventures opening themselves to potentially significant conflicts of interest? Should universities tolerate, support, or encourage scientists' dual relationships? The answers to such questions are beyond the scope of this study but, as noted in this review, the area of university-industry relationships and technology transfer certainly deserves further research to allow for more productive commercialization of new technologies and improved revenue streams to universities.

To date, relatively few universities have been able to turn this area into a significant source of revenue and co-operative research with industry, although indications reveal that this situation is changing.

The majority of the scientist-entrepreneurs in the study reported experiencing little support and even discouragement in dealings with their universities. Such experiences could, in the long term, be unproductive for both scientists and their institutions. These findings rely exclusively on the interviews with the scientists. For a more comprehensive understanding of this issue, technology transfer officials and other university representatives should be included in any follow-up study.

Scientists who are planning discussions with their institutions regarding technology transfer and entrepreneurial activities should prepare for such communications carefully, both in terms of content and contact. Certainly in-depth information about the university's position on these issues - what, if any, policies are in place, and who the persons are in the university hierarchy who formulate and administer these arrangements - should be obtained in advance of any formal approach. Reviewing the planned approach with scientists who have traveled this road before is also recommended for learning about this process.

The majority of the scientists expressed an interest in being able to maintain some relationship with the university after they initiated their entrepreneurial processes. One-third were able to do so. The continued relationships were mostly on a full-time basis with scientists having usually been able to structure their work with the ventures on a part-time basis to be compatible with their academic workload. In only one case was the scientist engaged on a full-time basis with the university while playing the role of the lead entrepreneur in the venture, and this situation tended to place both the person and the organizations under stress. Aspiring scientist-entrepreneurs can conclude from this finding that, in order to pursue both the venture and the academic career successfully, the most successful formula appeared to be the one where full-time university work was combined with a part-time function in the venture. This did not impede the scientist from a controlling role in the venture! Again the importance of carefully planning the role which the scientist wants to play, as discussed in chapter 5, is underscored.

In the area of comparative management, the research showed a tendency for Canadian scientist-started ventures to be better funded and supported through federal and provincial research grants and other programs than their counterparts in the United States. Both provincial and federal agencies in Canada appeared well organized in their support of high-tech research and venturing. This was highly valued by the scientist-entrepreneurs and was often reported to be a motivation contributing to the decision to start or continue a venture. However, at this early stage in the life of the venture, there was no indication that the more widespread availability of grants assisted Canadian firms in achieving higher organizational performance and at a faster pace than their U.S. counterparts.

Reference notes

1. Link, Albert N. and Tassey, Gregory "Editors' Introduction." In: *Cooperative Research and Development: The Industry-University-Government Relationship*, edited by Link, Albert N. and Tassey, Gregory. Boston: Kluwer Academic Publishers, 1989.
2. Geisler, Eliezer and Rubinstein, Albert H. "University-Industry Relations: A Review of Major Issues." In: ibid.
3. Ibid., p.44.
4. Buderi, R. "Universities Buy Into The Patent Chase." *The Scientist* , December 12, 1988.
5. Richter, Maurice N.,Jr. "University Scientists as Entrepreneurs." *Society*, July/August 1986.
6. Gosselin, Peter G. "Flawed study helps doctors profit on drug." *The Boston Globe*, October 19, 1988.
7. Etzkowitz, Henry. "Entrepreneurial Scientists and Entrepreneurial Universities in American Academic Science." *Minerva*, Vol. XXI, Nos 2-3, Summer-Autumn, 1983.
8. Dinces, Nathan B. "University Venture Funds." Paper presented at the 2nd Conference on Spin-off Corporations, Virginia Polytecnic Institute, Blacksburg, Virginia, May 1989.
9. Richter, op cit., p. 83.
10. Martin, Michael J. C. *Managing Technological Innovation and Entrepreneurship*. Reston, Virginia: Reston Publishing Company, Inc., 1984, p. 274.

Part III

Conclusions, Implications and Guidelines

Chapter 7

FINDINGS AND CONCLUSIONS

7.1 Introduction

The purpose of this research was to develop a *theoretical* and *practical* framework for the study of the scientist-started new business venture. In the implementation of this project, I aimed to identify and study the specific challenges and opportunities facing these kinds of start-up companies, and to suggest strategies for scientist-initiated ventures. This chapter summarizes the research project. It includes a reiteration of the conclusions reached and an evaluation of the propositions developed earlier in this study, and, finally, it presents a number of recommendations for further research. This chapter is laid out as follows:

7.2 Summary and Central Issues

The study explored key issues that appeared significant in the entrepreneurial planning and management processes of the scientist-started venture. The findings dealt with cultural and attitudinal characteristics, technology domination, opportunity assessment, team development and organization, university relationships, and government support. This section summarizes these findings and highlights the central issues.

7.2.1 Scientists' Orientations and Characteristics

Existing literature and research underscore the potential differences in cultural and behavioral backgrounds between scientists and other members of venture teams. The field studies among scientists and their partners generally confirmed these patterns and are summarized in these statements:

• Cultural and behavioral differences exist between scientists and managers, which is evidenced by their different perceptions of time and planning horizons, different value systems concerning money, management and control, technology development, and commercialization, and, consequently, substantially differing perceptions of organizational goals;

• Scientists' potential duality in loyalties in dealing with two different organizations; many are working for a greater cause (general scientific knowledge, the university) than just company objectives;

• Scientists' tendencies to be more objective and display greater skepticism and managers' tendency to appear to be more pragmatic and purpose oriented;

• Scientists' long-term orientation versus businessmen's short-term venture goals;

• The creative, eccentric, disorganized image of the scientist versus the administrative and control oriented manager;

• Scientists' tendencies to overrate the importance of technology in the venture as well as scientists' need for control over "their" technology as it transfers to the venture and is developed further;

• Narrow view of technology, that is, some scientists tending to see the technology as beginning and ending in the laboratory; the manager seeing technology merely as one of the many inputs in the commercialization process;

• Most scientist-entrepreneurs rating the need to advance and apply science as the primary motivation to start a venture.

The field studies also found important areas in which scientist-entrepreneurs did not differ from entrepreneurs in general:

• The scientists became entrepreneurs in the true sense of the word: they put their own resources at risk in the pursuit of a commercial opportunity;

• Scientist-entrepreneurs were also attracted to entrepreneurship in light of their needs to build businesses and obtain monetary rewards.

I have reiterated the characteristics here in detail as they constitute a critical element in understanding the scientist-started new venture. The remaining central issues to be discussed are all rooted in these differences in characteristics. In describing these issues, I used Adizes' **PAIE** model,[1] which was reviewed in chapter 2, in analyzing the various skill requirements of the early stages of the scientist-started venture.

7.2.2 Technology Domination of the Organization

Following the literature review, I concluded that the scientist-started venture can be expected to display a propensity to act in a technology-dominated fashion. Indeed, the field studies confirmed this notion. A strong technology orientation was observed to be a necessary, but not sufficient condition for achieving organizational performance goals. None of the observed research participants failed or faltered because of unsound technology. All the ventures that were researched focused on technology; those that had done so as an exclusive venture activity at the expense of other nontechnological tasks were often found to have stumbled in the areas of team integration, finance, administration, and marketing. Thus, the allocation of insufficient staff and resources to nontechnological functions in the scientist-started venture appeared to be a serious organizational trap.

7.2.3 Opportunity Assessment and Funding

Literature on entrepreneurial processes, such as works by Drucker,[2] Martin,[3] and Timmons,[4] stresses the early need for the lead entrepreneur's assessment of personal strengths and weaknesses as a basis for the evaluation of skills required in the venture. When I define the venture as the organizational structure that will facilitate the transformation of an idea into a commercialized opportunity, this implies that *assessment processes* need to be carried out at many levels, in an iterative fashion, to continually ensure that the venture is effectively converting ideas into opportunities. In the scientist-started venture, this need for assessment processes takes on a special importance. We have previously noted a propensity for the scientist-started venture to be technology dominated, and therefore to implement the scientific development from a more limited, technological perspective. The opportunity is not being comprehensively assessed if there is a failure to evaluate it from a fully multi-functional point of view, including the financial, marketing and distribution, development and manufacturing, and after-sales service perspectives. Only a quarter of the ventures reported completing formal market application assessments of their technology. While some kind of user feedback might have been solicited, the practice of formal market assessment did not appear to be customary for these kinds of ventures.

A broad-based assessment constitutes a critical requirement for the scientist-started venture given its propensity to a technology-push orientation and the generally longer development times and higher costs for science-based products or services. In view of the creative inputs required by the new venture in projecting all possible market applications, an openness is required to the use of *any* resources and expertise inside or outside the venture, to a thorough and ongoing assessment of the market, as well as to marketing, sales and distribution options and strategies.

Funding requirements often forced ventures into assessment processes in order to construct business plans. In funding, the potentially profound differences in value systems between scientists and the financial community were regularly exposed. This created tension between going along with the requirements of financial partners to achieve the venture's goals and the desire to independently pursue the application of science. In this light, a number of scientists, therefore, focused on grants or loans, even if it meant slower venture growth.

7.2.4 Team Building and Organization in the Venture

Although initial partners were sometimes selected from among the scientist's friends or colleagues, later partners and team members were primarily brought into the new scientist-started venture on the basis of their functional skills. This, in itself, is clearly sensible. However, once all the functionally required skills had been identified, team fit and interpersonal chemistry were often neglected. One would expect to find technological talents in these firms and one might furthermore encounter marketing and distribution talents, or in Adizes' terminology, Productive skills. One might additionally see some financial and administrative functions represented in Administrative skills. The founders, including the scientist, would usually represent the Entrepreneuring element. However, the element that pulls the team and resources together, the Integrative role, is frequently inadequately present or is missing entirely. This integrative function is pivotal in identifying and addressing the overall collection of skills required on the path from idea to successful commercialization. I believe that this function was called for when scientists and team members in the study mentioned that "professional management skills" were missing.

At some time during the development of their venture, most scientist-entrepreneurs admit implicitly or explicitly that they would benefit from learning about business, particularly in the areas of team and people management and finance. At the same time, this type of learning in basic management and business skills is not generally treated as a priority in the venture. One significant finding of this research is that scientist-entrepreneurs will recognize these needs but not act on them. This point is somewhat ironic since these technological and scientific entrepreneurs had reached their expert status through extensive training and experience in their fields of specialty, yet they expected to become successful businessmen without some basic business training. Although this issue has been only incidentally recognized in the literature, the findings of this study suggest that this problem is much more widespread than previously thought and much more critical to venture performance. Ventures that showed high organizational performance had fully or partially satisfied the need for these skills by assuring their presence in the venture team. In addition to the often quoted lack of time, this study did not uncover other reasons for this lack of commitment to business training. However, I believe that two additional factors could be considered and further researched. One is the belief that the need for business and management training can be satisfied by reading about these subjects. The second might lie in the scientist's continued ambiguity about the values of the business culture and thus an unwillingness to further embrace it.

Organizational structures themselves did not appear to cause problems in the scientist-started venture. Most ventures displayed informal, flexible organizational structures with few layers of management. Organization and management problems arose, not surprisingly, out of a technology domination which led to the absence of the required array of functional skills to exploit the opportunity. These problems also frequently occurred because of a lack of common values, goals, and planning horizons for the venture. This latter aspect could be explained by the often widely varying differences in professional cultures from which the venture team has been constituted, as well as by the lack of team management and integrative skills. To know about and be regularly updated on the founder's role and plans for the venture would further assist team members in clarifying their own roles and career plans.

7.2.5 Scientist-University Relationships

The relationship between the scientist and his university generally appeared to be difficult and tense. Even when considering the broader context of university-industry relationships, relatively few universities have been able to turn technology into significant sources of revenues and cooperative research.

The minority of scientists who reported positive relations with their universities dealt with institutions in which technology transfer and the outside activities of faculty had been clearly defined and communicated. Aspiring scientist-entrepreneurs should consider ascertaining their institution's objectives and policies in this regard, and learning about their practical implementation, before presenting formal proposals.

The majority of the scientists expressed an interest in maintaining a meaningful relationship with the university after they initiated their entrepreneurial activities. At the time of the study, one-third of the scientists maintained such relationships. These were all on a full-time basis with the university, and the scientists had been able to structure their work with the ventures in a way that was compatible with their academic workload. This particular model, which allowed a wide variation in the degree of control which the scientist chose to exert over the venture, seemed to be the most successful formula.

7.2.6 Government Support

My research identified one significant difference between Canadian and U.S. scientist-started firms. In comparing the various aspects of scientists' entrepreneurial activities in Canada and the United States, the evidence showed that Canadian ventures had, at some point, all received funding assistance through federal and/or provincial research grants, while in the United States, less than one third of the firms received (federal) grant support. In Canada, both federal and provincial agencies were observed to actively support high-tech research and venturing in non-monetary ways. The relatively widespread availability of these programs in Canada was reported to be a key motivation in the decision of the scientist to start or continue his venture. Although at this early stage in the life of the venture, the impact of support programs on organizational performance could not be discerned, the public policy implication is that government grants and assistance for bona fide high technology companies appear to positively influence the start-up decisions of scientists and their partners.

7.3   Evaluation of the Propositions

In chapter 2, I formulated a number of specific propositions to be tested. Although the issues concerned have already been discussed in this and previous chapters, I have, for completeness, evaluated these propositions here separately.

Proposition 1
During the planning and initial venturing phase of the scientist-started business enterprise, technology will tend to be overemphasized as evidenced through functional patterns in staffing, organization structure, and resource allocation.

As discussed in chapter 5, the study found this proposition to be confirmed in all respects.

Proposition 2
The scientist who in the formation and start-up phase of the enterprise, recognizes the cultural differences, that is, the lack of organizational skills and behavioral differences between scientists and managers, will be more successful in attaining business performance objectives.

In the concluding section of chapter 5, I described a number of ventures that had demonstrated better organizational performance than the remaining participants. None of the scientists in this study embarked on business or management training. However, all of the scientists in the high performing ventures had made an effort to expose themselves to such issues as funding and marketing strategies, and had attracted missing skills through deliberate team member selection. Four of these five high performers had clearly facilitated team formation and integration and assured commitment to common goals. This proposition thus appeared confirmed.

Proposition 3
Formal technological and market assessments by the venture team through a business plan in order to identify developmental needs and opportunities will improve the likelihood of early funding, effective technology development, and market exploitation.

In the initial stage of venture establishment, only five ventures had completed some type of market assessment activity. The demands of an effective management process and the funding requirements of running a new firm eventually inspired most ventures to carry out some form of assessment. All the high-performing ventures were characterized by scientist-entrepreneurs who had themselves questioned, or encouraged team members to thoroughly question, the technology in light of market opportunities. In these firms the scientist or another team member had, at some time in the life of the venture, established an appreciation of the market segment, and the motivation and modus operandi of potential customers. In the remaining ventures, it could also be observed that once technology and market demand were contrasted, if only informally, these companies became more successful in developing revenues. This proposition was confirmed.

Proposition 4
An informal but clear organization in the early stages of the venture to allow the balancing of entrepreneurial, productive, administrative, and integrative skill requirements, will create a climate conducive to attaining organizational performance objectives. Awareness of the potential pitfalls and opportunities of each stage in the life of the venture is valuable.

A difficulty in evaluating this proposition was the fact that, as the research proceeded in exploring specific areas of the scientist-started firm, the phrasing of the proposition increasingly appeared to be too general and raised issues that could not be addressed within the defined scope of this study. None of the organizations displayed formal, multi-layered, or bureaucratic structures. The organization *structure* did not, in this study, appear to be a variable in the functioning of these new ventures. In half the ventures, serious management problems did occur and they interfered with performance. I concluded from the findings of the study that these problems were predominantly rooted in the lack of common entrepreneurial objectives among the key members of the venture team. In contrast, the high performance ventures shared an organizational style that supported the development of a common vision, the need for professional management and non-technical skills, and attention to team chemistry, and integration. In terms of the need for a balanced presence of entrepreneurial, productive, administrative and integrative skills, this proposition appeared confirmed for the time periods studied. However, a fullfledged test of this proposition will require a review of organizational performance over a much longer time period to incorporate a more mature phase of the organization.

7.4 Further Research

Important variables that influence the performance of scientist-started ventures were identified in this study. Almost all areas covered by this exploratory study could benefit from some kind of further research. Additional studies could cover larger numbers of scientist-started ventures in the United States and Canada or in other countries such as those of Western and Eastern Europe. Longitudinal work measuring, a few years from now, how each of the present ventures evolved, would be attractive as well. On the basis of the findings of this work, I also developed a list of what I consider high priority research items that would significantly benefit the study of the scientist-started venture.

- A scientific study of scientists' psychological and other characteristics, especially those scientists who are also entrepreneurs, would contribute to the construction of a theory of the scientist-started new venture. An additional avenue for research might be the relationship between the scientists' psychological profiles and venture performance.

- A study focusing on the motivations of scientist-entrepreneurs in the area of management and business training could shed further light on the apparent conflict between need recognition and actions taken.

- Further explanatory research of the initial process of contrasting available skills with required tasks in the scientist-initiated firm; how does the resulting role distribution in the venture team influence organizational performance?

- The relationship between the scientist and his university has been studied in this project as an additional outcome of the entrepreneurial and organizational theme of this study. Further research in this area could benefit both the scientists and their universities in developing more effective relationships in entrepreneurial situations.

• An exploration of both scale and types of government funding for scientist-entrepreneurs as a policy tool to improve innovation.

7.5   Conclusions

At the outset of this book, I considered how the scientist-started new venture differed from other new ventures and whether any differences should be defined as a matter of nuance or principle.   I concluded that this type of new, high-technology firm is fundamentally different in the requirements it places on the venture team.   The early planning and management activities in the scientist-started venture require a perspective and application that is substantially different from the same processes in other new enterprises.   Specifically, the following conclusions are summarized:

• At the basis of many of the following comments is the finding that the scientist-started new venture attracts team members from an unusually wide array of fundamentally different backgrounds. Scientists can generally be expected to display significantly different attitudinal characteristics and cultural values than their colleagues in the entrepreneurial and business worlds. These differences appear in value attitudes towards scientific knowledge and development, business objectives, money and finance, management, control, management styles and planning horizons.

• When the resources of such a rich heritage of backgrounds and qualifications are efficiently organized and focused, as seen in a limited number of high performing enterprises, venture success in personal and business terms can be very rewarding.

• Scientists become involved in entrepreneurial activities through a mixture of motives including the application of science, the desire to build a business, and achieving monetary rewards. Scientists put their own money and resources at risk and are the most frequent source of start-up capital.

• Although differences in attitudinal characteristics and professional cultures are frequently recognized, few ventures consciously address the need for establishing a common culture which could bridge different values and objectives.

• Functional skills are often considered over team chemistry. Management conflicts frequently result and are rooted in a lack of common objectives among the team members, leading to reduced venture performance.

• Scientist-started ventures are often found to be heavily science and technology dominated in organization, management processes and resource allocation. The emphasis is on technology and other productive and entrepreneurial activities. Technology domination at the expense of other business activities impairs the venture's ability to develop in a stable and profitable fashion.

• Scientist-entrepreneurs tend to play entrepreneurial and technological roles in their ventures. They do not often play the integrative role of motivating the venture team and keeping it focused on common venture goals and mission. Those who do, or who facilitate other team members playing this role, positively influence organizational performance.

• Most scientists identify their personal need for business training in areas of team and people management and financial skills but none appear able to implement these personal plans.

• The majority of the scientists express a desire to maintain some relationship with the university but do not perceive their universities to be prepared for this option. The successful model appeared to be a full-time relationship with the university and part-time affiliation with the venture.

We are dealing here with a type of enterprise that is subject to continuous demands for rapid change, which is characteristic of entrepreneurship and new technology development. In addition, the members of these enterprises are from an unusually wide variety of cultural, attitudinal and functional backgrounds. If not addressed, this situation provides the potential for functional problems, interpersonal conflicts and, thus, organizational upheavals. It thus appears that the background of this type of venture and its members imposes an *intense* need for adaptation to common objectives. Seen from this perspective, it would be helpful for the founders of the scientist-started venture to specifically consider their enterprise as a *"learning organization."* Bomers[5] contrasts the classical organization and the learning organization as follows: "The basic building material of the classical organization is the task," and, "the building material of the learning organization, by contrast, is the team, which is formed by individuals and the qualities which they bring with them. The teams are self organizing in relation to the continuously changing and evolving tasks which they are facing." This ongoing learning approach is particularly applicable to the ventures we have studied. From the start, scientists need to become acquainted with the business and entrepreneurial cultures, and often need to train in business and management skills. Their partners also need to work at the formation of a common venture culture and often require technology training. Burns and Stalker[6] conclude that the "organic" organization is most conducive to a research and development based enterprise. The fluid nature of the organic model would facilitate the continuous adaptation to rapidly changing internal and external demands facing firms involved in high-tech innovation. I believe that in the context of the scientist-started venture, the concept of the learning organization complements the organic model in that it additionally suggests a commitment to learning and renewal for the venture organization in all its activities. Therefore, it may also be that by its very nature, the scientist-started, high-technology venture must remain in these organic and learning modes far longer than the typical young company.

In the field of innovation management, the study of the scientist-entrepreneur and his venture can further contribute to the transfer, application, and commercialization of science. The wider applicability of the research and its conclusions is based on the ability to generalize the input and output of this study. A key input has been the literature survey of cultural and attitudinal characteristics of *scientists in general*. Although the empirical section of this research focused on biomedical scientists and their ventures, there is no reason to believe that the conclusions of the study cannot equally apply to scientist-started ventures in other high technology fields.

Meanwhile, a number of the findings of this research can readily be translated into suggestions for the scientist-entrepreneurs and their partners in the development of their organization. Chapter 8 elaborates on a guide for aspiring scientist-entrepreneurs and their venture teams.

Reference notes

1. Adizes, Ichak. "Organizational Passages, Diagnosing and Treating Lifecycle Problems of Organizations." *Organizational Dynamics*, Summer 1979.
2. Drucker, Peter F. *Innovation and Entrepreneurship: Practice and Principles.* New York: Harper & Row, 1985.
3. Martin, Michael J. C. *Managing Technological Innovation and Entrepreneurship.* Reston, Virginia: Reston Publishing Company,Inc., 1984.
4. Timmons, Jeffry A. "New Venture Creation: Models and Methodologies." In: *Encyclopedia of Entrepreneurship*, edited by Kent, Calvin A., Sexton, Donald L. and Vesper, Karl H. Englewood Cliffs,New Jersey: Prentice-Hall, Inc.,1982.
5. Bomers, G.B.J. "De Lerende Organisatie." Paper presented at the opening of the academic year at Nijenrode Universiteit, The Netherlands School of Business, on September 4, 1989, Breukelen, The Netherlands: Nijenrode Universiteit, 1989, p. 30.
6. Burns, Tom and Stalker, G.M. *The Management of Innovation.* London: Tavistock Publications, 1966.

Chapter 8

A GUIDE FOR ASPIRING SCIENTIST-ENTREPRENEURS AND THEIR PARTNERS

8.1 From Scientist's Idea to Commercialized Opportunity

In this study, I analysed the scientist-started new venture in its early processes of translating scientific and technological ideas into applications and market opportunities. Although additional research topics were identified in the previous chapters, some of the current findings can already be applied in practice. This chapter will draw on these findings to propose some guidelines and checklists for aspiring scientist-entrepreneurs, their partners, and other interested parties, such as financiers, funding organizations, and universities. My purpose here is not to provide a general introduction to starting new ventures. Rather, the goal is to focus on the specific implications which arise when the scientist decides to become an entrepreneur. As a general background to scientific cultures, technological innovation, and entrepreneurship, works by Dubinskas[1], Martin[2], Roberts[3] and Timmons[4] can be used by the aspiring scientist-entrepreneur to develop an appreciation of these subjects. This will also allow the scientist to evaluate and test his specific motivation and commitment, before entering into the detailed activities demanded by entrepreneurship. Timmons, in particular, provides a wide array of practical exercises which may assist in early assessments of the entrepreneur's motivation and goals as well as the characteristics of the proposed opportunity. In this chapter, I therefore depart from the point where the scientist has reached the decision to explore entrepreneurial involvement in the commercialization of his scientific ideas.

The specific issues which face the scientist-started venture have been grouped below into five major, albeit overlapping activities and thought processes. Rather than repeat the particular background to each of these issues, the reader should, where required, refer to the previous chapters for further elaboration.

• Exploring the venture idea and considering technology transfer and employment issues with the university to arrive at a mutually satisfactory relationship with that institution.

• Bridging the cultural and attitudinal gaps among the team members to achieve commonly defined and accepted venture values, goals, and planning horizons.

• Assuring the balanced presence of all productive, administrative, venture integrative, and entrepreneurial skills at any one time in the development of the venture to support optimal organizational focus and performance.

• Supporting the notion of the scientist-started venture as a learning organization in which the team is self-organizing in order to to handle the continuously changing task requirements; training scientists in business skills and team members in fundamentals of the technology.

• Assessing the technological and marketing aspects of the development in the widest possible terms, counteracting the possibility for technology domination or the loss of opportunities not identified.

These five activity groups are interrelated and should be thought of as requiring concurrent and continuous rather than sequential implementation. Figure 8-1 shows a generalized flow of these activities to demonstrate what might typically be expected during the early development stages of the scientist-started new venture. The expected degree of intensity of these activities is represented by the grey areas in Figure 8-1. Of course this figure depicts an approximation since each individual venture is different and thus will present its own unique activity and timing requirements. I have used the Adizes model, described in chapter 2, to define the organizational stages from exploration to venture maturation.

Figure 8-1. Activities During the Early Stages of the Scientist's Venture

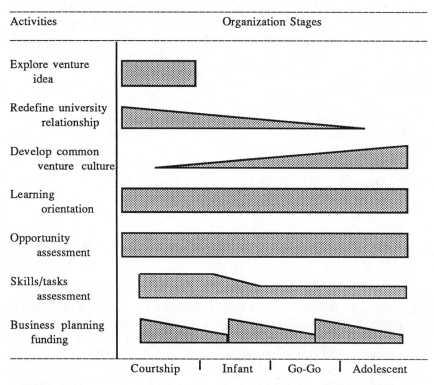

For each of these activities a checklist of items to be considered has been developed. Exploration of the venture idea and the development of the relationship with the university have been combined into one section. Business planning has been listed under skills and task assessment and development. The importance of business planning can hardly be overstated in terms of the resulting plan and for its iterative process, which invariably leads venture team members to a deepened understanding of the venture's challenges and opportunities. It is, however, outside the scope of this study to propose a detailed guide to business planning in general, and I refer to the many studies on business planning which have been published.

The checklists presented in this chapter are not designed as operating manuals, but rather aim to provide a reflective approach to the tasks of planning and

management of the scientist-started venture. Each venture is unique in its
characteristics and will require its own unique planning and implementation. In
the development of these guidelines, I have adopted the point of view of the
aspiring scientist-entrepreneur. However, the business and financial partners of
the scientist, as well as other concerned parties, may find issues in these
checklists which will complement their own preparations for going into
business with a scientist. This final chapter follows the outline of these
activities as follows:

8.2 Venture Exploration and the Relationship with the University
8.3 A Common Venture Culture
8.4 The Scientist-Started Venture as a Learning Organization
8.5 Skills and Tasks in the Venture Team
8.6 Opportunity Assessment
8.7 Concluding Comments

8.2 Venture Exploration and the Relationship with the University

Irrespective of the scientist's longer term objectives in relation to university
employment, the academic position can provide a secure platform from which
the venture idea can initially be explored, planned, and tested before any implementation takes place. In this exploration process, the desired long-term relationship with the university or research institution will, nevertheless, have to be
defined at an early stage, since that decision will influence many of the
subsequent activities that need to be planned and implemented. The following
items may guide this preparation process:

• scientist completes a self-analysis of strengths and weaknesses in relation to
  venturing
• review the strength and weakness analysis with trusted, objective third party
• identify the specific roles in venturing which appear most attractive to scientist
• identify the skills to be learned to fill such desired role; commit to training
• define the ideal long-term relationship with the university or research
  institution
• consider short- and long-term dependency on university salary and benefits
  structure

- initially explore what kind of partners and resources are required for venture
- become familiar with university technology transfer and intellectual property policies and how these might impact control over the subject technology
- study recent cases of technology transfer at the institution; interview scientists involved
- review availability and terms of university venture funds or other collaborative research programs
- investigate university policies and practices regarding conflict of interest and dual employment relationships
- become familiar with recent cases of scientists' involvement with commercial activities
- list specific items ideally wanted from the university in connection with the establishment of the venture
- define attractions which the venture might offer for the university
- strategize with trusted insider(s) in university affairs and potential venture partner(s) regarding alternatives with which to approach the university on technology transfer and employment issues
- approach university informally with entrepreneurship and employment ideas
- adjust plans as required; formalize venture plans and present to university and interested third parties

8.3   A Common Venture Culture

Recognition of the generalized picture of scientists' behavioral and cultural characteristics presented in this study can be of value in the early planning and management process of the new venture. The venture management team in this type of firm would typically be made up of individuals representing a wide array of backgrounds. This places a significant demand on the development *and* maintenance of a common venture culture which, in turn, will contribute to minimizing organizational upheavals and aid in focusing the young enterprise. Before moving to functional task and skills assessment, this section lists a number of issues of cultural significance which should be considered and *regularly reviewed* during the planning and early organizational phases of the venture.

- have the scientist define the initial venture mission and goals in terms of technology development, marketing vision, type of working style and venture team, business goals and funding sources, and monetary rewards

- review vision of venture mission with objective party and adjust as might be indicated
- review venture mission with (prospective) team member(s); compare all aspects, especially in terms of overall business values, planning horizons and partner's personal objectives
- review the specific roles in the venture which appear most attractive to scientist with team member(s)
- assess personality traits of (prospective) team members; use multiple interviews, references, and other input to evaluate personality match within the venture team
- ensure directly, or through a team member, that cultural differences within the scientist-started venture and the need for common values and mission are always recognized
- have the venture team develop and commit to clear venture mission and goal statements; assure frequent reviews of these statements
- present a clear and regularly updated statement of scientist-founder's role and goals in the venture to the team to enhance its perception of the ventures' mission and objectives.
- be aware, at all times, of which development stage the new venture is at in order to allow proactive management of anticipated challenges and opportunities
- carefully evaluate and verify, through references, the objectives and background of potential outside partners such as financiers, companies and consultants

8.4   The Scientist-Started Venture as a Learning Organization

I return here to the organizational style and emphasis which could benefit the scientist-started firm. This type of firm is subject to the dynamics typical of entrepreneurship as well as of new technology and, in addition, is made up of an unusually wide array of cultural, attitudinal and functional backgrounds. I believe that special attention to organizational attitudes is necessary to overcome the real possibility of a chasm opening up between the different cultures, and to effectively accommodate the technological and entrepreneurial changes of the project. A few areas of attention are recommended here.

- characterize the firm as a learning organization in which all members, individually and as a team, pay attention in all their activities to continuous adjustment to new opportunities and changed circumstances
- commit to and implement a program of *orientation and training in basic business and management skills* for the scientist-entrepreneur and other technical team members to enhance venture team abilities
- consider a fluid organization for optimal internal and external adaptation to change
- let the venture management team itself play a role in organizing the distribution of team tasks and skills
- support an active venture team orientation towards maintaining extensive contacts outside the venture in all functional areas to foster the creation of new opportunities for the enterprise
- train nontechnical team members in the basic principles of the technology to enhance the venture team's ability to manage and promote the innovation

8.5 Skills and Tasks in the Venture Team

To highlight the importance of common venture mission and goals, I separated, for purposes of presenting this chapter, the team dynamic and cultural issues from those regarding specific functional skills. In the development of a venture team, these two aspects need to be integrated when identifying needed skills. Considering the tendency towards technological domination of early venture activities, the identification and attraction of a balanced set of functional skills, commensurate with the requirements at any particular stage of the firm's development, needs careful attention.

- recognize all functions-- technical and nontechnical--as contributing equally to the venture's goals
- plan for the venture team with the objective of providing balanced functional skills
- be aware of the tendency to under-allocate staff and resources to nontechnical areas
- let the scientist and the initial venture team develop a list of required functional tasks
- consider technological development, production, marketing, distribution, finance, funding administration, business planning, and integrative and team

management requirements
- review the tasks-skills assessment with outside business experts or mentors for feedback
- evaluate the task list in light of the skills already available in the team
- determine the balance of functional skills required and at which stage in the firm's development
- evaluate the feasibility of allocating tasks among full-time, part-time or contract sources of required skills
- assure the presence of integrative skills to effectively motivate and mold a team towards common venture goals and objectives and their achievement
- produce and regularly update a business plan, even if not required for funding purposes
- project the image of a functionally well balanced and professional venture team

8.6   Opportunity Assessment

How does the scientific or technological idea translate into a successful commercial opportunity? What particular implications are there in this process for the scientist-started venture? One tendency noted in this study was that of technological domination leading to insufficient exploration of the market opportunities. On a wider basis, the entire field of opportunity assessment from all perspectives presents a challenge for the scientist-initiated new enterprise. Opportunity assessment is also a key ingredient in the business planning cycle and will influence the success of funding drives. Early in the life of the venture, the state of the technology needs to be communicated to all members of the venture team and, without disclosing proprietary detail, to outside technological and marketing experts, and possibly to government officials in case of grant applications. A number of items are proposed here which may assist in the development of an effective opportunity assessment process.

- recognize the fact that the scientist may no longer be objective about the technology
- accept the notion that research and development requires skills different from those of production
- emphasize the need for the entire venture team to understand and support the technology
- produce an initial assessment and description, in layman's terms, of the

technological state of the idea
- establish a venture technology review group representing the widest area of functional skills
- recognize that technological and marketing optimization might be beyond the skills of the venture, in view of the unknown applications and development needs of the innovation
- find access to and accept the use of outside advice to contribute to the opportunity review process
- apply iterative review processes to the technology to contrast it with existing and imaginable potential uses
- find access to or develop comprehensive market research information
- invite early user feedback about major aspects of the initially proposed products and/or services
- evaluate alternative applications of the technology in terms of their impact on the venture's objectives
- allow adjustment of the technology development plans as indicated by the review process

8.7 Concluding Comments

One of the areas to which limited specific attention was paid in part III relates to funding. This reflects the fact that while funding is an important and integral part of science-based venturing, it usually results from a successful coming together of the other elements discussed in this book. When venture and business planning, common venture cultures, balanced functional skills and opportunity assessment are addressed effectively, funding is usually achieved by the venture, as was borne out by the high performers in the field studies.

The recommendations and checklists of this chapter have suggested a number of steps and orientations which may aid the venture management team in the successful planning and development of the venture. These items are based on the findings of this study as well as my own experiences in working with such enterprises, and they incorporate especially those particular challenges and opportunities which typically face the scientist-started firm.

Reference notes

1. Dubinskas, Frank A. "Janus Organizations: Scientists and Managers In Genetic Engineering Firms." In: *Making Time, Ethnographies of High-Technology Organizations.* Edited by Dubinskas, Frank A. Philadelphia: Temple University Press, 1988.
2. Martin, Michael J. C. *Managing Technological Innovation and Entrepreneurship.* Reston, Virginia: Reston Publishing Company, Inc., 1984.
3. Roberts, Edward B. and Fusfield, Alan R. "Staffing the Innovative Technology-Based Organization". *Sloan Management Review*, Spring 1981.
4. Timmons, Jeffry A. with Smollen, Leonard E. and Dingee, Alexander L.M.,Jr. *New Venture Creation, A Guide To Entrepreneurship.* Homewood, Illinois: Irwin, 1985.

BIBLIOGRAPHY

Acs, Zoltan J. and Audretsch, David B. "Editors' Introduction." *Small Business Economics* , Vol. 1, No.1, 1989.

Adizes, Ichak. "Organizational Passages, Diagnosing and Treating Lifecycle Problems of Organizations." *Organizational Dynamics*, Summer 1979.

Adizes, Ichak. *How to Solve the Mismanagement Crisis.* Santa Monica, California: Adizes Institute, 1979.

Altus, William D. "Birth Order and Its Sequelae." *Science* , Vol.151, January 7,1966.

Bartunek, Jean M. and Betters-Reed, Bonita L. "The Stages of Organizational Creation." *American Journal of Community Psychology*, Vol 15, No.3, 1987.

Bomers, G.B.J. "De Lerende Organisatie." Paper presented at the opening of the academic year at Nijenrode Universiteit, The Netherlands School of Business, on September 4, 1989, Breukelen, The Netherlands: Nijenrode Universiteit, 1989.

Buderi, R. "Universities Buy Into The Patent Chase." *The Scientist* , December 12, 1988.

Burns, Tom and Stalker, G.M. *The Management of Innovation.* London: Tavistock Publications, 1966.

Campbell, Joseph, with Moyers, Bill. *The Power of Myth*, New York: Doubleday, 1988.

Danielson, Lee Erle. *Characteristics of engineers and scientists, significant for their utilization and motivation.* Ann Arbor, Michigan: Bureau of Industrial Relations, University of Michigan,1960.

Deutsch, Claudia H. " Staying Alive in Biotech." *New York Times*, November 6,1988.

Dinces, Nathan B. "University Venture Funds." Paper presented at the 2nd Conference on Spin-off Corporations, Virginia Polytecnic Institute, Blacksburg, Virginia, May 1989.

Drucker, Peter F. *Innovation and Entrepreneurship: Practice and Principles.* New York: Harper & Row, 1985.

Dubinskas, Frank A. "The Culture Chasm: Scientists and Managers in Genetic-Engineering Firms." *Technology Review*, Vol. 88, May/June 1985.

Dubinskas, Frank A. "Janus Organisations: Scientists and Managers In Genetic Engineering Firms." In: *Making Time, Ethnographies of High-Technology Organizations* , edited by Dubinskas, Frank A. Philadelphia: Temple University Press,1988.

Etzkowitz, Henry. "Entrepreneurial Scientists and Entrepreneurial Universities in American Academic Science." *Minerva*, Vol.XXI, Nos. 2-3, Summer-Autumn, 1983.

Geisler, Eliezer and Rubinstein, Albert H. "University-Industry Relations: A Review of Major Issues." In: *Cooperative Research and development: The Industry-University-Government Relationship*, edited by Link, Albert N. and Tassey, Gregory. Boston: Kluwer Academic Publishers, 1989.

Gosselin, Peter G. "Flawed Study Helps Doctors Profit on Drug." *The Boston Globe*, October 19, 1988.

Greiner, Larry E. "Evolution and Revolution as Organisations Grow." *Harvard Business Review*, July-August 1972.

Kerlinger, Fred N. *Foundations of Behavioral Research*, New York: Holt Rinehart and Winston, Inc.,1973.

Link, Albert N. and Tassey, Gregory "Editors' Introduction." In: *Cooperative Research and Development: The Industry-University-Government Relationship*, edited by Link, Albert N. and Tassey, Gregory. Boston: Kluwer Academic Publishers, 1989.

Litvak, Allan Isaiah and Maule, Christopher J. "Some Characteristics of Succesful Technical Entrepreneurs in Canada." *IEEE Transactions on Engineering Management*, Vol-EM 20, no 3, August 1973.

Martin, Michael J. C. *Managing Technological Innovation and Entrepreneurship*. Reston, Virginia: Reston Publishing Company, Inc., 1984.

Miles, Matthew B. and Huberman, Michael A., *Qualitative Data Analysis*. Beverly Hills: Sage Publications,1984.

Moss Kanter, Rosabeth. *When Giants Learn To Dance*. New York: Simon and Schuster,1989.

Paulin, William L., Coffey, Robert E. and Spaulding, Mark E. "Entrepreneurship Research: Methods and Directions." In: *Encyclopedia of Entrepreneurship* , edited by Kent, Calvin A., Sexton, Donald L., and Vesper, Karl H. Englewood Cliffs, New Jersey: Prentice-Hall,1982.

Richter, Maurice N., Jr. "University Scientists as Entrepreneurs." *Society*, July/August 1986.

Roberts, Edward B, "Influences on Innovation: Extrapolations to Biomedical Technology." In: *Biomedical Innovation*, edited by Roberts, Edward B., Levy, Robert I., Finkelstein, Stan N., Moskowitz, Jay and Sondik, Edward J. Cambridge, Massachusetts: The MIT Press, 1981.

Roberts, Edward B. "What We've Learned: Managing Invention and Innovation." *Research-Technology Management*, Vol 31, Jan/Feb 1988.

Roberts, Edward B. and Fusfield, Alan R. "Staffing the Innovative Technology-Based Organization", *Sloan Management Review*, Spring 1981.

Roberts, Edward B. and Peters, Donald H. "Commercial Innovation from University Faculty." *Research Policy*, No. 10, 1981.

Roberts, Edward B. and Wainer, Herbert A. "Some Characteristics of Technical Entrepreneurs." *IEEE Transactions on Engineering Management*, Vol EM-18, no 3, August 1971.

Simon, Jane. "The New Breed." *New England Business*, October 20,1986.
Sindermann, Carl J. *Winning the games scientists play*. New York: Plenum Press,1982.

Sindermann, Carl J. *Winning the Games Scientists Play*. New York: Plenum Press, 1982.

Skinner, Wickham. "Technology and the Manager." In: *Readings in the Management of Innonvation*, edited by Tushman, Michael and Moore, William, L. Marshfield, Massachusetts: Pitman Publishing Inc.,1982,

Timmons, Jeffry A. "New Venture Creation: Models and Methodologies." In: *Encyclopedia of Entrepreneurship*, edited by Kent, Calvin A., Sexton, Donald L. and Vesper, Karl H. Englewood Cliffs,New Jersey: Prentice-Hall, Inc.,1982.

Timmons, Jeffry A., with Smollen, Leonard E. and Dingee, Alexander L.M.,Jr. *New Venture Creation, A Guide to Entrepreneurship*, Homewood, Illinois: Irwin, 1985.

Van Brunt, Jennifer. "Executive Hiring Trends: Entrepreneurs and Managers." *Bio/Technology*, Vol 6, September 1988.

INDEX

About The Author

Karel J. Samsom is a native of The Netherlands, where he completed a degree in Economics at the University of Groningen. In the late sixties, he moved to the U.S. and earned an MBA from The Wharton School of Finance and Commerce (University of Pennsylvania). Recently, he received his Ph.D. from Nijenrode Universiteit, The Netherlands School of Business.

Karel J. Samsom has worked internationally in the fields of finance, business planning, organizational restructuring, market evaluation and new venture development. Within these functional areas, his overriding emphasis in building effective organizations has been, and remains, on developing well integrated management and new venture teams. He has worked as a consultant with Towers, Perrin, Foster & Crosby, and as an executive and venture manager with Eli Lilly and Alcon Laboratories. Starting in 1986, as its president, he led Psychemedics Corporation, a scientist-started biomedical venture, through its founding, public offering and initial commercialization processes. During the last 20 years, he has lived in Belgium, Britain, California, France, Indiana, Pennsylvania, Switzerland and Texas. Now based in Vermont, Dr. Samsom is active in teaching, research, and business in North America and Europe, with a special emphasis on funding, organization and technology transfer in technology-based new enterprises. Karel J. Samsom is himself a practicing entrepreneur and is also a partner in Samsom Good Associates, a consulting firm in Burlington, Vermont. His research and teaching activities focus on entrepreneurship and the application of science in industry and he is affiliated with Nijenrode Universiteit, The Netherlands School of Business, the University of Vermont, School of Business Administration and Saint Michael's College, Graduate Business Studies, in Vermont